GW00646306

PILLOW LACE

The Lace Maker
by *Netscher*

PILLOW LACE
A PRACTICAL HAND-BOOK

BY ELIZABETH MINCOFF, Ph.D.

AND

MARGARET S. MARRIAGE, M.A.

WITH ILLUSTRATIONS BY ERNEST MARRIAGE
AND FIFTY PATTERNS

RUTH BEAN

CARLTON · BEDFORD

1981

Originally published by John Murray, London, 1907.

Reprinted by permission of the copyright owner.
Ruth Bean, Victoria Farmhouse, Carlton, Bedford MK43 7LP, England.

Distributed in the U.S.A. by Robin & Russ, Handweavers,
McMinnville, Oregon, 97128, U.S.A.

ISBN 0 903585 10 3
Reprinted 1981

Printed in Great Britain at the
University Press, Cambridge

PREFACE

OF late years there has been a marked revival in England of interest in pillow lace; not the interest of the collector in old laces, the historical interest, which has always continued without regard to fashion, but interest of a more practical kind. To this revival fashion in dress no doubt contributed, but its real root lies more in the growing respect for handicrafts, and the cultivation of village industries induced by the cry of "Back to the land." This change of attitude has not yet been reflected in the books on lace published in England; with the exception of a few pamphlets and the advertisements of thread-makers, they all treat the subject from the standpoint of the collector.

Some years ago, when on a holiday at Freiburg in Breisgau, we learnt the elements of Torchon from a young Czech. On returning to England we had the greatest difficulty in finding any new patterns from which to work. We found valuable articles by Mme. Amélie Olivier in "La Mode Pratique," but the laces there given were usually not easy, and the French technical terms used were not to be found in any dictionary. For the English learner of pillow lace nothing was available but some pamphlets on the elements of Torchon, with simple ordinary patterns;

after that meagre instruction she was left to sink or swim by herself. We therefore planned this book with the object of giving a thorough and graduated course of instruction in the easier kinds of pillow lace. We have endeavoured at the same time to bring the means of further progress within the worker's reach by the suggestions contained in Chapter IV, and by the glossary of technical terms at the end of the book, which will enable any one possessing an ordinary knowledge of French or German to work from the foreign books mentioned in the bibliography.

Writers on pillow lace have used various systems for explaining the working of patterns. Some have had recourse to a code of symbols of the most discouraging appearance ; some have merely given prickings of patterns with scanty explanations ; in other cases the explanations are so long that they weary and confuse the reader. Our ideal has been to make the explanations as short as possible, relying to a great extent on the diagrams, which show clear and detailed direction lines and indicate all the difficulties, and the difficulties only, by number. To avoid repetition, we have chosen a carefully graduated set of examples. The book cannot be begun at random. The worker may start with either Russian, Torchon, or Maltese, but should take the laces of the chapter chosen in their order, and should not attempt Chapters X and XI without having mastered at least Chapter IX.

Our readers may be interested to learn that while this book was being written, some of the chapters in the manuscript were lent to a beginner, one of the staff of the East Anglian Sanatorium at Bures, who wished to teach some of the poor women patients lace-making, so that they might have an occupation and at the same time earn some money. With a little supervision, she learnt Russian lace from them in less than a week.

In a work of collaboration it is difficult to assign to the workers their respective parts; it may be sufficient to say that I am responsible for the first six chapters, the rest of the book being shared between Mrs. Marriage and myself.

We desire to acknowledge our indebtedness to the Hon. Rose Hubbard, of the Winslow Lace School, for kind permission to reproduce the lace shown in Fig. 23, and to make and publish a pattern of the handkerchief border No. 26. Our thanks are also due to Messrs. Hachette and Co. for permission to reproduce pattern 43, and to Messrs. Ponting Bros. for leave to photograph various implements.

ELIZABETH MINCOFF.

Sofia, Bulgaria,
      April, 1907.

CONTENTS

LIST OF ILLUSTRATIONS

PILLOW LACE

CHAPTER I

THE ATTRACTIONS OF LACE-MAKING

Qui trop embrasse, mal estrainct.

AS a handicraft, pillow lace-making offers such attractions that, at first sight, it seems strange so few Englishwomen should take to it. The real reason for this neglect is that lying at the root of the degeneration of all Englishwomen's handicrafts, for to them the odious term "fancy-work" is often most appropriately applied. Not that this degeneration is now at its lowest ebb ; on the contrary, of late years embroidery patterns have frequently borne evidence of some intelligence and knowledge of the principles of design, and the colours employed have been far less insipid than formerly.

The Royal School of Art Needlework at South Kensington has produced excellent results, as have the Manchester School of Embroidery and the London Guild of Needlework. The movement known, by a strange inversion of terms, as "art nouveau" in England, and as "modern style" in France, has, with all its contortions and undeniable perversities, put new life into the art of embroidery and has practically created that of stencilling on textiles.

But what is really needed to regenerate women's handicrafts is a change in the standpoint of the workers.   They should take their crafts a little more seriously.   Granted that these are, to the vast majority, merely agreeable pastimes, on which to spend stray hours of leisure, still no artistic result, no result really worth having, can be attained if these stray hours are spasmodically devoted now to drawn thread work, now to crochet, and then to leather or poker work.

It is this diffusion of work and ingenuity that has led to the neglect of pillow lace as a home art.   For pillow lace involves some study and requires learning ; the tools are unfamiliar to most of us, and the technique is quite unlike that of needlework, being more akin to weaving—another woman's handicraft also relegated to the professional worker.

But, after all, the learning needed is not very formidable ; a few simple turns of the bobbins, once thoroughly understood and remembered, form the key to the most intricate laces.   And from almost the very first the worker is making something really desirable ; the narrowest, simplest lace looks well as the edging to a frill or the finish to a piece of embroidery.

Almost any handicraft will yield, not perhaps works of art, yet specimens of really good craftsmanship, if pursued by itself and with patience.   And the time spent will be more pleasantly spent as the worker obtains greater mastery over her materials. The shorter the leisure at the disposal of an amateur, the more need she has for concentration in such pursuits if the result is to be worth having. This applies equally even when occupations of this kind are regarded purely as recreation ; for any handicraft worthy the name always offers enough variety to keep all but the most fickle and uncertain of workers well amused when once it has appealed to her taste. Pillow lace is certainly a handicraft of this kind, great in its scope and variety. It brings into play not only the dexterity, but also the ingenuity of the worker in adapting and altering patterns. Old pattern-books[1] contain many valuable suggestions and long-forgotten designs which are fascinating to work out. And more than ingenuity is brought into play if the worker should aspire to invent new patterns or adapt such designs from embroidery, tiles, wrought-iron work, etc., as may lend themselves to the purpose. For the designing of a pillow-lace pattern demands far greater skill and technical knowledge than does that of a pattern for point lace. There is not only beauty of line to take into account, but also the strength of the fabric, and this involves much care in rightly placing and balancing the threads. The field before the pattern-maker is very wide, and improvements are sorely needed. If any one would introduce new patterns with bold decorative curves, or other really effective designs with a character to them, to take the place of the debased rococo flowers and

---

[1] See Bibliography, p. 224.

wearisome geometrical figures that we know too well, all lace-makers—to say nothing of the vast numbers of those who wear lace and whose houses are embellished with it—might well be grateful.

But even without aspiring to the invention of new designs for broad laces, beautiful effects can be obtained by the adaptation of existing patterns. A narrow insertion may be modified to go round great curves, thus forming a bold design, and let into some linen cloth. There are also possibilities for combinations of shaped tapes woven on the pillow in all their curves and applied on net, or joined with needle-point stitches. All these possibilities await the ambitious.

And for the least ambitious, the least self-reliant of workers, pillow lace offers other attractions. It makes no demands on that sense of colour which is, unfortunately, so singularly rare in our countrymen, as one has to admit with a blush when one looks at and admires the embroideries of Bulgarian peasants, or watches the skill with which a Moorish servant arranges daring and gorgeous effects among the flowers on a dining-table. It seems as if sense of colour were, like sense of smell, refined away by civilization.

Then, again, so long as you work correctly there is no likelihood of the lace produced being of bad quality ; that is the outcome only of crass carelessness and hurry. Aim at an even tension, no very difficult thing to attain, follow the lines of your pattern accurately, set your pins firmly and straight, and your lace cannot fail to be well made from the very outset.

It is most encouraging for the beginner to find everything looking "so professional" from the first. There are no dull parts in the work (as in embroidery the stems of the flowers) ; all is almost equally interesting. And there is no better employment to keep one from fidgeting while listening to conversation or to reading aloud, since there is no counting to be done, and the work can be taken up or dropped at any moment, for one cannot "lose the place."

Once the initial cost is defrayed, it is the least expensive of handicrafts, entailing only the cost of the thread, which gains infinitely in value in the worker's hands. And the initial outlay is small enough : bobbins, winder, and stand should not cost together much over ten shillings ; the other things the worker can either make or probably possesses already. This making something well worth having out of really raw material has a great satisfaction in it. I remember an old Yorkshire farmer saying of drawn-thread work : "You lasses mun be allus pulling summat to pieces. It's fair waste o' good stuff." And, after all, there is something to be said for the criticism from his point of view, but it does not apply to pillow lace.

To some, lace-making may appeal as a picturesque pose ; but without owning to such a weakness, any sufficiently human woman will, other things being equal, prefer a handicraft that has pretty, dainty accessories. The bright pillow, the quaint bobbins, the many-coloured pins are undeniably attractive. They are not a litter in the room, but an ornament.

In summer too, when to many needlework is a doubtful joy, entailing effort with a sticky needle and the frequent use of emery cushions, the smooth wooden bobbins are delightfully cool to handle. The position of the lace-maker is more comfortable than that of the embroideress, who is forced to tire either hands and arms with holding up her work or else her back with bending over it. Lace requires an easy upright position. I knew a dyspeptic who always worked at her lace pillow for half an hour after meals, and this obligatory upright position had the best effect on her health.

So much for the pleasures of making lace ; there are besides the pleasures of possessing what one has made. There are so many uses for the finished product that the lace-maker is never likely to be in the position of, say, the basket-maker, who has soon provided herself and all her acquaintance with as many baskets as they will want for years to come. The lace you make will never go out of fashion. It drapes beautifully, falling into far more graceful folds than does point lace. If good thread is used and solid patterns chosen, it will resist endless washing. Here, again, it wins a victory over most "points." At the risk of being called a Goth, I must protest against the theory that no lace should ever be ironed. Most pillow laces—all described in this book —are all the better for being ironed while damp, nor will a little starch hurt in most cases.

A far worse prejudice is the one against frequent washing of lace. Nothing is improved by dirt, certainly not anything that is worn on the person and even near the skin. It seems to me that on calm reflection soiled lace can be nothing short of disgusting, and that it should be admired " Isabella colour " or dipped in tea to make it look old, foxed, and mildewed is incomprehensible. Any one who has inherited lace from some one with these ideas knows to her cost how impossible it is to remove the yellow stains, a mark of the dirty habits of the last owner. Lace is far more likely to be spoiled by letting it get really dirty, when the fabric has to be rubbed hard to cleanse it, than by more frequent careful washing. Of course it should be washed very gently. Simmering long and gently in a solution of some mild soap will be found to cleanse it with the minimum of rubbing ; it is friction that most hurts it.

Since we are speaking of prejudices, let me say that there are few subjects about which more absurd prejudices are rife than this very subject of lace, and in few is tradition more blindly followed. Lace is admired far more often for its age, the cost of production, its name's sake, than for any intrinsic beauty. The magic words Mechlin, Valenciennes, Brussels, are passports to admiration even for the most banal of patterns ; and laces of the Revolutionary period do not need to be pretty in order to be prized, and that not merely as curiosities, which is natural, but as works of art.

We should try to clear our minds of this slavish worship of authority and be conscious what it is we admire. Is it the bold curves of the pattern, the pleasant suggestions of some quaint piece of "pot-tenkant" with its trim flower-pots, the flowing intricacy of Russian labyrinths, the texture and the light graceful folds of Chantilly, or the richness of Brussels?

> One may do whate'er one likes in Art.
> The only thing is to make sure
> That one does like it, which takes pains to know.

And so in lace. There are so many styles, so many different ideals of beauty, but let us feel sure that an example has reached a point some way along the path to *one* of these ideals before we blindly admire it.

CHAPTER II

HISTORICAL SUMMARY

Il n'y a rien de nouveau dans ce monde que ce qui est oublié.
(Saying of Marie Antoinette's milliner.)

THE origin of lace is, like most other origins, wrapped in mist, to dispel which many legends have arisen, more or less picturesque, more or less improbable. There is the legend of its Venetian birth ; of the love-sick girl who, gazing hour after hour at the coral her sailor had given her as a keepsake, came to imitate its slender and intricate branches with a mazy weft of linen threads.

Flanders from all time has disputed with Venice the invention of pillow lace, and one Flemish tradition is that the last Crusaders on their return from the Holy Land brought the industry to the Low Countries. Another, that of Bruges, has it that lace was suggested to a Flemish lover by the sight of a cobweb on his sweetheart's apron.

From Brabant they say it was carried to Nuremberg in the bundle of a Protestant refugee, escaping from Spanish persecution. A rich burgher's daughter of Nuremberg learned the art, and on her marriage introduced it into her Saxon home. She taught the daughters of her husband's miners to make lace, and the name of Barbara Uttmann came to be revered round Annaberg for her industry and for the welfare brought by her means to the whole district of the Erzgebirge. It was foretold her on her marriage that she would have as many children as there were bobbins on her lace-pillow, which came true, runs the story, for at her death she had seventy-five children and grandchildren. So if we trust tradition we must conclude that the lace Barbara made was either rather narrow, or else of the kind known nowadays in Germany as Idriaspitze (cf. chapter vii), for on other laces thirty-seven pairs make only a poor show. This Barbara is a less mythical figure than the Venetian fisher-girl who precedes her. We know the dates of her birth and death (1514 and 1575), and the epitaph on her tombstone at Annaberg announces that she "invented" pillow lace in 1561. If she invented it, she was not the first to do so, as the two volumes of lace patterns called "Le Pompe," published at Venice in 1557 and 1559, show already an advanced stage in the development of technique. However, in the face of all this detailed information,[1] and of the lady's statue set up centuries later by the still grateful town of Annaberg, we cannot dispose of her too summarily. She belongs with William Tell to the borderland between history and legend.

The story of the introduction of the lace industry into the English Midlands by Catherine of Aragon during her retirement, while awaiting her divorce, at the dower-house of Ampthill Park, in Bedfordshire,

[1] Rasmussen, p. 5 f.

might be true. A pattern named after her is still in use in the district,[1] and further to confirm the story it is said that till the beginning of the nineteenth century St. Catherine's Day (25 November) was kept as a festival by the lace-makers in her honour. But this comes rather as a contradiction than as confirmation, for St. Catherine was, to her cost, poor lady, the patron saint of wheels, and among others of spinning-wheels. To this day the Protestant peasants of the Palatinate spin during the winter months from Catherine's Day to Candlemas, and on Catherine's Day a fair of spinning-wheels is still held at Neckargemünd, near Heidelberg. One cannot but suspect that the Queen's name was brought in to explain a Catholic survival in a Protestant district.

The account of the twelve venerable Westphalians,[2] who taught lace-making in Tondern in 1647, is not incredible, curious though it be. They were chosen for their skill by an enterprising citizen to teach any who should apply to them. Their beards were so long that while they worked they were forced to keep them in bags out of the way of the bobbins and pins.

All these stories doubtless have their grain of truth, even the tale of the coral, for the earliest pattern-books for pillow lace hail from Venice, and Venice has from the earliest times of lace been known as a great head-quarters of the industry. The first Venetian patterns are said by competent authority[3]

---

[1] See the photograph in Channer and Roberts, p. 19.
[2] Rasmussen, p. 7.
[3] Séguin, and " Edinburgh Review," 1872, p. 49.

to have an Oriental character in the arabesques that form their designs. This and the fact that the very first published patterns show a fully developed technique make it seem to me probable that the art of pillow lace-making was introduced into Venice from the East by one of the many channels at the disposal of that great commercial power; for at the time when we can first accurately date pillow lace in Venice the Venetians were the carriers of Europe. Had it been a native growth, we should probably have seen more tentative, clumsy beginnings, both in the pattern-books and in the specimens of old Venice lace still surviving, not the graceful, complex designs that lie before us. Only some one well acquainted with the intricate history of the Oriental textile arts can bring the final proof or refutation of this theory. But if for the present there is no decisive proof of the Eastern origin of pillow lace, at least the evidence is strong in its favour. The Flemish legend of the Crusaders bringing the art from the Levant gives its slight weight on this side, but far more important are the facts that we find an art with Oriental patterns starting almost simultaneously in the three chief seaports trading with the East—Venice, Genoa, and Ragusa—and nowhere else in Europe.

Another theory, plausible at first sight, is that the pillow-lace industries in different countries had separate origins, all derived from the primitive art of plaiting. When, however, we take into account the technical uniformity of all European pillow lace, it is difficult to believe in a theory involving separate

origins. Even fabrics so different in character as
Valenciennes, Russian, and coarse Cluny are formed
of the same stitches and can be made with the same
tools. Then again, though plaited threads or cords
had been used for trimming all through the Middle
Ages, there are no traces of lace before the end of
the fifteenth century, and these first traces are more
than doubtful. Actual specimens of lace of course
bear no evidence of exact date. Pieces have sometimes been made depicting some event; one, for
instance, has portrait heads of Queen Victoria,
Prince Albert, and their two eldest children;[1] but
such specimens are altogether exceptional, and could
not occur in primitive laces owing to their technical
difficulties. Even such evidence of date cannot be
implicitly accepted, as a very elaborate piece of needle-
point, representing the defeat of the Armada and
Tilbury Fort among dolphins and flags and English
roses,[2] must for its technique belong to the eighteenth,
or at earliest to the late seventeenth century.

One frequently sees pieces of pillow lace in museums
ticketed as belonging to the fifteenth century or
as older still;[3] these tickets are pure romance. According to some authorities, the first traces of pillow
lace occur in pictures and in certain inventories of
linen belonging to the D'Este[4] and other great Italian
families from 1476 onwards. As to the inventories,
they must be accepted with great caution. There
occur in them Latin terms which seem certainly to

---

[1] Bury Palliser, p. 264.   [2] *Ibid.*, p. 396.
[3] For instance, in the fine collection at the Gruuthuis in Bruges.
[4] Bury Palliser, p. 46; Dreger, p. 24.

refer to bobbins and pillows ; but the bobbins may
have been only some kind of reel to hold cord for
plaiting, and the pillows may have been used, as
indeed they often were, for embroidery.   One of the
great difficulties in dealing with such descriptive lists
or with the old pattern-books is to arrive at a really
clear understanding of the dozens of technical names
rife in the fifteenth and sixteenth centuries for every
kind of needlework.   The historical side of these
subjects has mostly been dealt with by men, or by
women unversed in their technique, which has led
to continual confusions.   One may go so far as to
say that barely half a dozen of all the writers on the
subject of lace are capable of distinguishing the old
printed patterns for needle-point from those used for
pillow lace ; while, on the other hand, those who have
practical knowledge have seldom the learning or in-
clination to make researches in archives or museums.
It seems almost too absurd that repeatedly references
to lace, in the sense of shoelace, staylace, etc., should
have been hastily set down as proof of the existence
of points and guipures, but so it is.   Even the
British Museum Catalogue exhibits an instance of
this carelessness.   The library contains three manu-
scripts relating to the plaiting of narrow braids by
hand, the latest of which (1651) bears the appropriate
title of " The Art of Making Strings," and has a
specimen of each silken string, from one-eighth to a
half-inch broad, neatly stitched down beside the instructions.   Yet the oldest, a fifteenth-century production, is endorsed as containing a treatise on lace

and has often been brought up as an authority.   The
inventories then must be taken as evidence only with
caution.   As to the pictures, in several cases a pillow
with some leaden weights attached to it, no matter in
what way, has been accepted without further criticism
as a lace-pillow.

If pillow lace was made at all in Europe before
1520, it certainly was not in common use until some
thirty years later.   Portraits of the reigns of Henry
VIII, Edward VI, and Mary[1] in England, and of
Francis I[2] in France, bear no trace of lace.   The
earliest French portrait showing lace is said to be
that of Henry II at Versailles; the ruff is edged
with a very narrow and simple pillow-lace edging.
Whereas from that time onwards French portraits
offer a rich and valuable source for lace patterns.
Our own Elizabeth and her courtiers are in their
portraits loaded with lace ; and while at the beginning
of the seventeenth century Dutch artists constantly
introduce it even in religious subjects, very little
occurs in their pictures before 1580.[3]

The introduction to " R. M's " pattern-book, published at Zürich by Christoff Froschower[4] about the
year 1550, gives us clear proof that pillow lace was
known in Venice before 1526.[5]   It says : "The art of

---

[1] A. M. S., pp. 11-12.   [2] Séguin, p. 11.

[3] According to Séguin, none ; but the lady in the portrait by Pourbus, dated
1551, in the Municipal Museum at Bruges, wears three kinds of lace, one of
which was certainly made on a pillow, and possibly two.

[4] Printed verbatim in Ilg's "Geschichte und Terminologie der alten Spitzen,"
p. 31.

[5] This date is misprinted (1536) by Mrs. Bury Palliser and by Ernest
Lefébure.

pillow lace (*die kuenst der Dentelschnueren*) has been known and practised for about twenty-five years in our country, for it was first brought by merchants from Venice and Italy into Germany in the year 1526." Causes other than the first discovery of lace by Venice merchants, during their journeys in the East, may have timed its spreading in Europe from Venice at this particular moment. Severe sumptuary laws repressed the wearing of gold, silver, jewellery, cloth of gold, silks, and other materials of value. In this delicate product of plain white thread lay an admirable chance of evading them and gratifying the natural taste for luxury and artistic beauty in dress. Again, without metal pins, or with only a limited number of them, not much could be achieved in the way of pillow lace. In England, during the reign of Henry VIII, the price of ordinary pins was about a penny each in our money; and although on the Continent they were in common use, they seem to have been somewhat of a luxury until the second half of the sixteenth century.

The first known pillow-lace patterns of certain date are those already mentioned of the collection called "Le Pompe" (see Fig. 1), published at VENICE in two volumes in 1557 and 1560. Both volumes fortunately are accessible to Londoners, the first in the edition of 1559, a copy of which is in the Victoria and Albert Museum, the second in a reprint of the 1562 edition published by the Imperial Austrian Museum at Vienna in 1879.[1] Together they form a rich and

---

[1] Publisher, F. Paterno.

FIG. I. A PAGE FROM "LE POMPE," 1559 EDITION

FIG. 2. A PAGE FROM PARASOLE'S "TEATRO," 1616

beautiful collection of geometrical patterns which, as M. Séguin points out, have no relation to the general style of Renaissance art, but for the most part take their inspiration from the East. All the patterns are for pillow lace ; the great majority are plaited laces, some varied by the introduction of small squares or circles of grounding ; there are also tape laces. These last are of great interest as disproving a theory, that was held with much apparent reason, that the process of "crochetage"[1] originated in Flanders, where it has always been held in especial favour. The Pompe patterns show us this process well established. It is difficult to give any adequate idea of this work, which in variety and in the charm and simplicity of its designs far surpasses any of the other old pattern-books that I have had opportunity to see.

On working out a number of the most original and representative of the patterns in this book — the plaited laces—I found them, as a rule, too stretchy for modern needs. They were meant, not for insertion or edging, but for sewing on to the seams of coats, etc., and unless supported by a foundation fell out of shape at once. However, two of them, with slight alterations, are included among the working diagrams in the chapter on plaited laces ; they are Nos. 33 and 34.

No one in Italy seems to have published any more pillow-lace patterns until 1591, when Cesare Vecellio brought out a large and important work in four parts,

---

[1] See below, p. 94.

called the "Corona."[1] It ran through a number of editions, the last appearing in 1608. Most of the patterns are for point lace, and those which could be worked on a pillow are so little specially adapted to this technique that they too may well have been intended for points.[2]

In 1597 Elisabetta[3] Catanea Parasole brought out her first collection of patterns at Rome, called "Studio delle virtuose dame."[4] They are thirty-three charming designs, but serve our purpose very little, as only two narrow and insignificant edgings to other laces are for the pillow. Elisabetta mentions on all her title pages that the designs are of her own drawing. As a designer she has strength and great power of invention, and the methodical arrangement of her books is an admirable contrast to the confusion in those of her male colleagues, this owing no doubt largely to her technical knowledge and their ignorance of the crafts for which they designed. Each technique is treated separately ; patterns for drawn thread, reticella, and point lace are ranged in groups. Her next book, the "Pretiosa Gemma delle virtuose donne," was published at Venice in two parts, 1600–1,[5] and reprinted at Rome in 1610

[1] Reprinted by Wasmuth, Berlin, 1891.

[2] They are six in all : in Part I a narrow insertion, the second from the bottom on page F 4 ; another in Part II on GG 4, above the picture of Vesta (repeated in Part III, GGG 4) ; in Part III the broad guipure on CCC 4, and two narrow insertions, DDD 2, the bottom but one to the right, and the lowest on GGG 1. Part IV has one narrow insertion, CCCC 1, the lowest to the left.

[3] Or Isabetta, or Isabella, for she gives herself all three names.

[4] Reprinted by Quaritch, London, 1884.

[5] Reprinted by Ongania, Venice, 1879.

and 1625.[1] The first part contains point and reticella
patterns, the second, besides these, darned net and two
broad pillow laces which show lack of experience in
handling bobbins.   Indeed, were it not that in her
methodical way she has indicated the number of
bobbins required, few would take the patterns to be
for pillow lace.

Her "Teatro delle nobili et virtuose donne" (see
Fig. 2), published at Rome in 1616,[2] shows enormous
progress in the pillow patterns.   Evidently pillow lace
had come more into fashion, and the artist herself
gained mastery over its technique.   There are seventy-
four pillow patterns of great variety of style, many
beautiful and some most elaborate.   In most cases
the number of bobbins needed is given, varying from
fourteen to a hundred, while the laces are of all
widths up to about four inches.   All are geometrical
in design and of light fabric, the majority, very light
indeed, consist of twists and plaits.   They are of the
guipure order, if we use the word in its present meaning ; that is to say, the fabric is formed by the design
itself without the aid of grounds.   These patterns
have not the same happy art as those of "Le Pompe"
in producing effect by the skilful variation of different
simple methods.   They are more monotonous, more
complex, less practical.   But they are far better
arranged, and evidently this kind met with greater
success, for both Mignerak and Shorleyker publish
quite similar patterns, while I have seen no attempt

[1] Strange, "London Bibliographical Society Trans.," VII, 235.
[2] Reprinted by Wasmuth, Berlin, 1891.

to revive the style of "Le Pompe." The present
representative of Elisabetta Parasole's laces is Cluny,
a name at first given to modern copies made at Mirecourt of certain old laces in the Musée Cluny at Paris,
but now extended to a number of geometrical guipures.

Besides being the birthplace of the lace industry
as far as Europe is concerned, Venice manufactured
great quantities of lace, chiefly needle-wrought, but
some pillow laces, until into the nineteenth century.
At the present day lace is no longer made in Venice
itself, but at two places near by, Burano and Pelles-
trina. Both industries were reorganized about the
year 1872 to relieve the distress consequent on a
terribly cold winter. Now Burano alone employs
four hundred workers.[1]

Directly after the rise of lace-making at Venice, we
find it established at GENOA, and whereas Venice for
the most part produced point, Genoa chiefly developed
pillow lace. The little leaves which have been likened
to grains of millet[2] are of Genoese origin, a later
development brought about by the change in fashion,
which introduced the flat, turned-down collar in place
of the quilled ruff. The ruff demanded a light,
graceful lace, which all its frilling could not make
heavy (see Figs. 3, 4), and for this the first Venetian
patterns were admirably adapted. But these laces
looked poor and flimsy on the new collars ; something richer and heavier was needed (Fig. 5). The
curves of the pattern were now formed by tapes

---

[1] An interesting account of the Burano lace school is given in the "Century
Magazine," XXIII, 333.   [2] See p. 95.

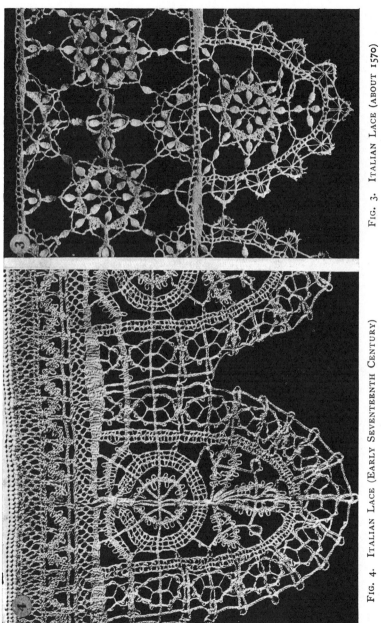

FIG. 3. ITALIAN LACE (ABOUT 1570)

FIG. 4. ITALIAN LACE (EARLY SEVENTEENTH CENTURY)

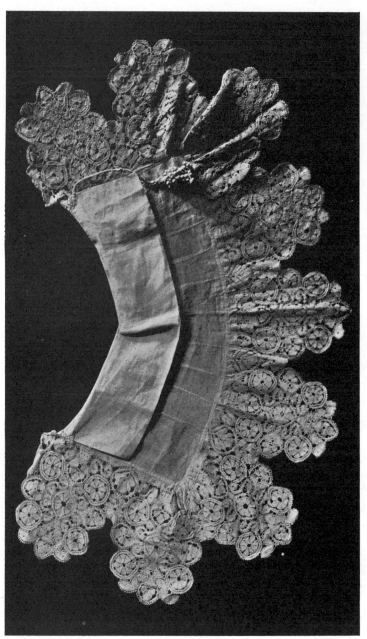

Fig. 5. Flemish Collar (First half of Seventeenth Century)

Fig. 6. Italian Insertion (Seventeenth Century)
Fig. 7. Milan Point (reduced) (Seventeenth Century)

FIG. 8. A PAGE FROM DANIELI'S PATTERN BOOK, ABOUT 1640

instead of plaits (Fig. 6), and these leaves or bars were introduced, probably from reticella (then a very fashionable form of needlework), where they play a most essential part as "bullion stitch." This heavier Genoese lace was made from about 1625 onwards. Its lineal descendant is modern MALTESE, which was introduced into the island by lace-workers brought from Genoa in 1833 by Lady Hamilton-Chichester, wife of a governor of Malta. Though Genoese by extraction, the industry, flourishing exceedingly in Malta, has developed a character of its own, retaining as essential the Genoese leafwork, but very little of its solid tapes, light twists taking their place. Characteristic is also the Maltese cross in the patterns and the cream or black silk in which the lace is usually worked. There is besides some fine thread Maltese lace and a great deal of Torchon made in the island. Great quantities of coarse guipure are made nowadays near Genoa at RAPALLO, and all along the coast from Albissole to Santa Margherita. The patterns have charming boldness and originality, but in the specimens I have seen both workmanship and material left something to be desired.

MILAN early learned the industry from Genoa, evolving a marked style in its productions. Point de Milan (Fig. 7) has copied the Genoese tape guipure, but substituted the Valenciennes ground for the connecting *brides* of the original. It is one of the earliest grounded laces. At the present time the lace trade of the district is carried on at Cantu, near Lake Como.[1]

BOLOGNA distinguished itself as the place of pub-

[1] Bury Palliser, p. 66.

lication of Bartolomeo Danieli's pattern-books, two
of which are in the Victoria and Albert Museum,
both dating about 1640.   Nearly all the patterns are
for points, but the last page of one volume is devoted
to most beautiful "Russian laces" (see Fig. 8).
Lace is still made in Bologna, where there is a school
of lace.   There are others at Coccolia near Ravenna,
Udine, Pisa, Florence, and Perugia.   Friuli and
Naples also have lace industries.

Of the lace made at RAGUSA we have very little
information, although it was one of the first, and very
celebrated in its day.   In the little town that is now
all that remains of the great Slavonic Republic,
which for a century or more disputed the commercial
supremacy of Venice herself, gold lace is still produced.   The "point de Raguse,'" so often mentioned throughout the seventeenth century, may have
been gold lace also, but we have no certain data.
Louis XIV, after Ragusa had sided with Austria
against him in 1667, forbade all importation of
"point de Raguse" into France.   The present lace
industry at Idria and that which in the eighteenth
century flourished at Laibach, might, being on Slav
territory, have taken their origin from Ragusa; but
the nearness of Venice and the fact that Laibach has
always spoken German, not Slavonic, point rather
to a Venetian source.   There are at present State-
supported lace schools in the neighbourhood at Idria,
Isola, and Chiapovano.[2]

[1] We need not assume that "point de Raguse" was needlework, despite its
name, for "point de Milan" is pillow-wrought.

[2] Brockhaus, "Conversations Lexicon," art. Klöppeln.

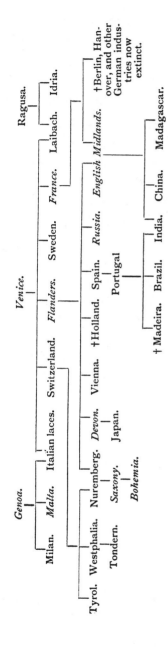

NOTE.—The places printed in italics are the most important lace-making centres. In those marked † lace has ceased to be made.

If these industries are of uncertain origin, there are many others which undoubtedly spring from Venice. Indeed, Venice is the mother or grandmother of all European laces except those just mentioned. Her eldest daughter is one of the least important. SWITZERLAND, though it still makes a good deal of Torchon as a peasant industry in the district between Neufchatel and Basel, never excelled in pillow lace from the time when the art reached its full development. But the Swiss interest in lace during the sixteenth century is proved by the publication of three pattern-books—one at Zürich about 1550, another at St. Gall by Georg Straub in 1593, and a third six years later by Ludwig Künig at Basel. Straub's pattern-book is a reprint of Part III of Vecellio's "Corona."[1] Künig's designs are Vinciolo's darned net patterns. But the Zürich pattern-book of "R. M.," published by Christoff Froschower, and now surviving in the libraries at Vienna and Munich, is a most important source. Ilg[2] reprints the introduction verbatim, and very interesting it is. The author begins by stating "the art of pillow lace-making (*die kuenst der Dentelschnueren*) has been known and practised for about twenty-five years in our country, for it was first brought in the year 1526 by merchants from Venice and Italy into Germany.[3] . . . Clever women and girls, admiring it,

---

[1] See above, p. 18.

[2] "Geschichte und Terminologie der alten Spitzen," p. 31 f.

[3] This word is not to be understood in its present political sense, but as meaning wherever the German tongue was spoken, including much of Switzerland and Austria.

contrived with great industry and zeal to copy and
reproduce the same . . . and invented new models
much more beautiful than the first." In technique
also the Swiss workers made such progress that the
author says, "In my opinion the art has now reached
its highest point." There was a growing demand
for the new product, and women "could earn a
better living at lace than with spindle, needle, shuttle,
or anything else of the kind," and the number of
lace-makers greatly increased. "At first these laces
were only used for shirts,[1] but now they have come
to be used on collarettes, round the necks of bodices,
on sleeves, caps, as edgings and bindings, on and
round aprons and barbers' cloths,[2] on handkerchiefs,
table and other linen, pillows and bedclothes, beside
many other things which I need not mention. . . .
Years ago, when quilting and raised work was in
fashion, it took more time than I can tell for a
seamstress to make a collarette, or the edging round
the neck of a bodice, or such-like, to the great
expense of those who employed her in their houses.
Now a lace can be bought cheaply and sewn on in a
few minutes, and the greater part of the expense
spared. When collarettes and the like were worked
with gold and silk, people were put to a great expense
to wash them with soap : this is now saved, for all
these laces being of flax thread can very well be
washed with lye." Our author is eminently practical;

---

[1] i.e. shirts and shifts, whether for day or night wear, and camisoles. Some
of the following terms in dress are obsolete and difficult to render exactly.

[2] Or according to Dreger, "coarse cloths."

perhaps "R.M." is the cover for some good house-
wife shrinking from publicity, but to this the book
gives no clue; the only fact divulged is that "R.M."
has taught lace-making in Zurich for twelve years.
The fruit of this experience is given not only in the
patterns, but in suggestions for making broader laces
by means of parallel repetitions of any given pattern,
and for varying them by the use of coloured threads.
Of the patterns themselves some examples may be
seen in Dreger's "Geschichte der Spitze";[1] they
resemble the more elementary and least successful
patterns of "Le Pompe" for plaited laces.

The Swiss lace industry received a fresh impetus
from the incoming of French Huguenots after the
Revocation of the Edict of Nantes in 1689. They
settled at Geneva, and to the double exasperation of
the Grand Monarch smuggled lace made not only
abroad, but by the heretics he had expelled, back
into his own territory over the passes of the Jura,
which were too inaccessible to keep under surveil-
lance.

Besides the Torchons already mentioned, narrow
laces are still made at Neufchatel, with a fine net
ground and thick flowers, resembling Lille lace, an
unattractive variety that has been made banal by
machine copies, and which thickens terribly in
washing.

It is a question how far the peasant industry in the
TYROL and the former lace trade in NUREMBERG were
the outcome of this of Switzerland. For the Tyrol

[1] Sixteen are given.

we have no data; Nuremberg is traditionally supposed
to have been taught by Flemish refugees from Alva's
persecution, which is quite likely. In the Germanic
Museum of that city there are specimens of pillow
lace made by a Nuremberg lady about the year 1600
from Vinciolo's patterns.

Infinitely more important is the pillow lace of
FLANDERS; indeed, it is in this district that pillow
lace ranks the highest as an industry, employing the
greatest number of workers and producing laces of
the highest grade. This fact, coupled with a natural
patriotic feeling, has led Belgian writers to claim for
pillow lace a Flemish origin, which is, however, dis-
proved by the later appearance of Flemish laces.
According to Séguin, the Low Countries did not start
making lace before the arrival of the Duke of Alva in
1567, and from that time until the death of his master
Philip II the sufferings of the unhappy country would
not have favoured the starting of such an industry.[1]
This I hold to be an overstatement of the case, for
the Pourbus portrait of 1551, already mentioned,[2] is
of a Flemish lady in very Flemish surroundings, and
her clothes are decidedly trimmed with lace ; nor are
they so recherché, nor in any other way different from
those in other Flemish portraits of the time, that we
need assume them to be imported. But whether this
is so or not, there is distinct evidence that Flemish
lace was later than Italian, in the fact that Flanders
published no pillow-lace pattern-book until that of
Jean de Glen at Liége in 1597, and de Glen in his

[1] Séguin, pp. 191, 131.   [2] p. 15.

preface himself says that he brought his patterns from Italy. They are a transcript of Vinciolo. Early Flemish laces are copied from Italian models,[1] and more especially from those of Genoa. At first the lighter Genoese style was imitated, the plaits ornamented with leafwork; but soon Flemish taste found its natural bent in the solid, massive patterns of the later Genoese. The original Genoese patterns were mostly based on the use of parallel tapes, which were woven into each other as they were formed. The great change brought into these laces by the Flemings was the substitution of a single tape for three or four and the use of "crochetage"[2] to form the fabric. But this cannot be the *invention* of the Flemings as M. Séguin has it, for as we have already seen "Le Pompe," the earliest Venetian pattern-book, has many designs which necessitate crochetage. This does not, however, prevent that process from being characteristic of Flemish laces, for in them it plays a far more important part than in any others save Russian, which doubtless were copied in the first place from Flemish models. Early seventeenth-century guipures of Flanders and Brabant often consist of a single tape even for the broadest lace, and this tape is not greatly varied as in modern Bruges or Honiton; it is of the same weaving and pretty much of the same width through the whole of its course, and runs unbroken throughout the lace (Fig. 10). The system of crochetage has to this day remained a marked characteristic of Flemish guipures. It was long before French

[1] Ilg, p. 41.　　　[2] See p. 94.

FIG. 9. ITALIAN LACE (SEVENTEENTH CENTURY)
FIG. 10. FLEMISH LACE (ABOUT 1630)

Fig. 11. Flemish Lace with Shallow Scallops (Eighteenth Century)

FIG. 12. FLEMISH LACE WITH STRAIGHT EDGES (SEVENTEENTH CENTURY

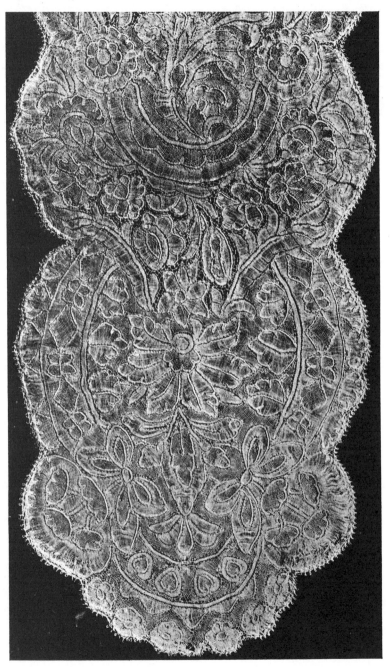

FIG. 13. BRUSSELS LAPPET (EIGHTEENTH CENTURY)

lace-makers learnt the process, not indeed until Colbert imported Flemish workers into France in 1665, and it has never become popular in that country.[1]

The Flemings further varied their laces by substituting shallow scallops (Fig. 11) for the deep Vandycks of their models. Later these scallops became flatter and flatter until the nearly straight edges (Fig. 12) of Mechlin and Valenciennes were evolved. Early seventeenth-century Brabant guipures show wonderful boldness and beauty of design ; carnations and other flowers are conventionalized in graceful curves of the tape with the greatest success. The eighteenth century brought greater technical skill, such skill as will never be surpassed (Fig. 13) ; but the designs do not show the same improvement, and by the nineteenth century they had little by little degenerated into the naturalistic flower-pieces of modern Brussels. Some of the finest eighteenth-century guipures were made at Binche, which no longer produces. Brussels has always been their chief centre, especially for the finest kinds ; Bruges produces a great quantity, mostly of coarser workmanship ; Ghent and St. Trond also make guipures.

Quite a different style of lace ran parallel with the guipures from about the middle of the seventeenth century. The need for a cheaper lace suggested the scattering of heavy *motives* of the guipure order, filling in the intervening spaces with a light groundwork of net, which took less time to make than the thick parts or *mats*. Such laces draped better in folds,

[1] Séguin, pp. 39-40.

being lighter; but these folds concealed the pattern, and as less attention was given to the design, it deteriorated. So we come to the exquisite workmanship of MECHLIN and the banality of its patterns. Mechlin and Valenciennes are the two principal Flemish laces of this class—the *dentelles à réseaux* or grounded laces. They are worked to and fro across the pillow, ground and flowers together, which necessitates the use of a great number of bobbins— 500 is no uncommon number, for very fine thread is used. Had we never heard of the high prices paid for Mechlin lace, this fact alone would prove that while the origin of these grounded laces lay in an effort at cheapness and simplicity, the new variety soon ranked with Brussels itself in price and quality. It was at its best during the first half of the eighteenth century. It is made in Mechlin itself and at St. Trond and Turnhout. It is more elaborate than Valenciennes, and has a far greater variety of stitches (Fig. 14). The trade of late years has fallen off owing to the fact that Mechlin has been copied by machines with especial assiduity and success.

The same applies to VALENCIENNES (Fig. 15), but this lace, being in its most usual forms cheaper, has resisted better. Its patterns have adapted themselves more successfully to changes in taste, while Mechlin clings to its rococo designs with the greatest tenacity. Valenciennes washes and wears excellently well, and however clever the machine copies may be, they never reproduce the texture or the durability of the real thing. It is made most in the district between

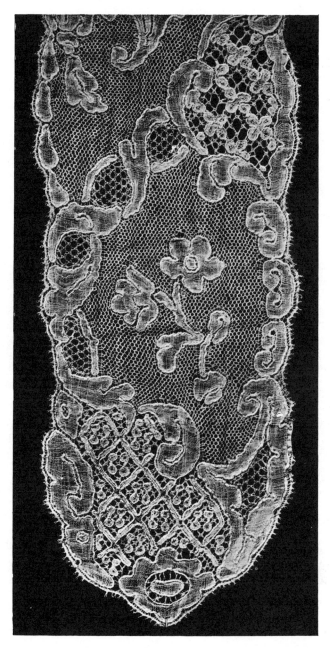

Fig. 14. Mechlin Lappet (First half Eighteenth Century)

Fig. 15. Valenciennes Lace (Eighteenth Century)
Fig. 16.   ditto   (Nineteenth Century)

Poperinghe, Courtrai, and Ghent,[1] also at Valenciennes, Ypres, Alost, and Bruges. In the latter place the convent lace schools make little else, and one of these alone has 420 pupils. These convent schools are not a pleasant sight; most of the little girls have a dazed, stultified look, that very naturally would come from spending hours cooped up with eyes fixed on the fine threads.

During the last thirty years[2] Valenciennes has had a new development—the Brabant variety (Fig. 16), which is worked differently, the thick parts first separately, the background being afterwards worked on to them. These laces are often extremely handsome.

Antwerp formerly made and exported quantities of lace to South America via Cadiz; but that market being closed, the industry has died down except for local use in peasant costumes. The favourite style of pattern was "pottenkant," i.e. "pot-lace," so called from the flower-pots on it, which are said to be a reminiscence of the kind of flower-pot almost always present in old pictures of the Annunciation.[3]

Black silk laces are made at Grammont, Enghien, and Oudenarde.[4]

HOLLAND never seems for any length of time to have followed the example of her sister State as to lace, even though more than once French workers took refuge in that country. Such lace as was made there seems to have been needlework.

---

[1] A. Lefébure, p. 160.　　　[2] *Ibid.*, p. 161.
[3] Bury Palliser, p. 130; Ilg, p. 44.　　　[4] Bury Palliser. p. 134.

WESTPHALIA probably learnt the art of lace from her Flemish neighbours. There is, I believe, no trace there to-day of the old industry, though in the neighbouring Rhine province the artistic activity of Düsseldorf has produced a modern revival of lace. But Westphalia must have been a centre of the lace trade, for in 1647 Westphalian workers were introduced into TONDERN in Schleswig by a merchant of that town anxious to improve the local lace, which had already been making some thirty years. In 1712 Tondern's lace-makers were reinforced by Flemish women who had followed King Frederick's army from the Netherlands. The industry was at the height of its prosperity during the early years of the nineteenth century. The Flemish character noticeable in the old specimens has given way to that of Northern France and Malta. Tondern is the only place in the old kingdom of Denmark where there ever was a trade in lace, and one of the few in the German Empire where it has survived. It has been said that Venice lace, taking an overland route to Flanders, had left traces behind in Cologne and Augsburg,[1] patternbooks being published in both towns ; but it will be found, I think, that the books in question contain no pillow patterns. The only German patternbook for which I can vouch that it contains pillow patterns is Wilhelm Hoffmann's "Gantz new Modelbuch" of 1607, which gives sketchy indications of seven insignificant narrow edgings for the embroideries which are the main object of the book.

---

[1] Cole, "Cantor Lectures," p. 8.

Hoffmann had published another set of patterns for cutwork in 1604, but these have no pillow lace among them. The same applies to all the fine works of Hans Siebmacher and to the whole of the very fair collection of old German pattern-books in the Victoria and Albert Museum.

The earliest German lace centre is the one still by far the most important, that of the ERZGEBIRGE, which from Saxony has spread into Northern Bohemia. Of the legend concerning this industry we have already spoken. It is more probable that Barbara Uttmann learned what she knew from the Swiss during her girlhood at Nuremberg, teaching her new neighbours at Annaberg after her marriage. There is no reason, as several have done, to explain away Barbara's lace as netting, since we have seen[1] that pillow lace had been common in Switzerland at least twenty years before her marriage, and a commercial city like Nuremberg was bound to have trade relations with the Swiss. There are besides traces of lace industry in the seventeenth century at Nuremberg.[2] Information about the lace trade in Germany during the sixteenth and seventeenth centuries is very scanty; but there is proof that about the year 1660 the industry was widely spread, in the following extract from J. G. Schoch's "New Poetical Pleasure and Flower-Garden," Leipzig, 1660, which also shows us in what esteem it was held by the cultivated classes: " It is sad to see how common our poems are become nowadays, in what contempt they are held, when

---

[1] See above, p. 24.   [2] Bury Palliser, pp. 264, 44 ; Ilg, pp. 35, 37.

such fine and excellent songs not only go the rounds of all the village alehouses and taverns, but are even to be found pinned to every lace pillow." We have no trustworthy information about the SAXONY lace trade until 1666,[1] when we hear of it spreading over the Bohemian frontier to Grasslitz. The Revocation of the Edict of Nantes brought Protestant French lace-workers to Saxony, and to Prussia, Hanover and Hesse besides. Lace never greatly prospered in those parts, but in Saxony it kept on gaining ground, until in the eighteenth century we hear of Dresden and Meissen laces. In 1766 the Empress of Austria tried to make it spread further on the Bohemian side by offering prizes, and a school was endowed at Prague for the purpose of copying Belgian laces, but the enterprise failed because it was not run on sound commercial lines.[2] After the French Revolution emigrants again stimulated the Saxon trade by introducing lace-making into Leipzig and Halle, besides starting new industries in Hamburg, Berlin, Anspach, and Elberfeld. Berlin alone had at one time 450 workshops.[3] None of these remain to-day, but the Saxon trade is as great as ever. From 1808 to 1817 four State schools for lace were started in Saxony; at present there are twenty-eight, with a special school for pattern-designing at Schneeberg.[4]

French writers constantly affirm that Saxon laces cannot compare with theirs for quality, that design, workmanship, and material are alike inferior. This

---

[1] Ilg, 36.   [2] *Ibid.*   [3] Bury Palliser, p. 264.
[4] Brockhaus, "Conversations Lexicon," art. Klöppeln.

may be true as far as Saxon copies of fine French laces are concerned ; but there is a variety of guipure made in the district,[1] sometimes of soft glossy thread, sometimes of coarse cream-coloured silk, of quite distinctive charm. The patterns, though not geometrical, are very conventional, and a good deal of raised work is made on the *mats*, in the shape sometimes of stars, sometimes of sprays of leaves.

A great deal of Torchon is produced, of all qualities, besides Cluny and Maltese. In the winter men work Torchon as well as women, and are supposed to make it better, their tension being usually tighter. The lace-makers have a curious way of amusing themselves by repeating long rhymes, somewhat in the style of "Mother Hubbard" or the "Ten Little Nigger Boys," setting their pins by the rhythm or by the numbers in the rhyme. One is about the cuckoo with thirty wives, and what they each did, another about the twelve geese who stole oats, and so forth. The lace-makers keep count of the number of pins set during the recital and see who has done most work in the time.[2]

Beside the Erzgebirge there is no other lace trade of importance in Germany. Of late years the institution of art trade schools has influenced lace, notably in Düsseldorf, a great centre for the applied arts.

As to AUSTRIA, there is the old industry in Croatia already mentioned, and one in the Tyrol, with four

---

[1] See chapter XI.

[2] These rhymes are given in Alfred Müller's "Volkslieder aus dem Erzgebirge," 1891, p. 214.

State-endowed schools at Proveis, Luserna, Predazzo, and Calavino. Besides these, a central school at Vienna is devoted to the making of new patterns. This school has published the best, and so far the only scientific manual of lace, a great folio work by Carl Jamnig and Adelheid Richter. It is a collection of beautiful photographs of plaited and Russian laces, progressively arranged with clear explanatory notes.

The Austrian industry long kept in touch with Belgium. Vienna attracted lace-makers from Flanders, while both were under the same government, and in the middle of the eighteenth century the Emperor Francis summoned the sisters van der Cruyce from Brussels to teach lace-making there.[1]

The peasants in HUNGARY make "Russian" laces, but probably more for home use than for commerce; for though we see specimens in museums, no Hungarian town figures as a trade centre.

Of far greater consequence is the lace trade in FRANCE, for nearly half of the total half-million of lace-makers in Europe are French.[2] It was also one of the first countries to make lace, learning in all probability direct from Italy in the middle of the sixteenth century. The pedlars of Auvergne fetched most of their wares from Italy and travelled far and wide in France, carrying their stock-in-trade on their backs, and in company with their wives and children. Séguin[3] traces to them the introduction of

---

[1] Ilg, 37.

[2] Bury Palliser, p. 188; it should be remembered that these figures refer not only to pillow lace, but to points.   [3] p. 22.

the lace trade into Auvergne, le Velay, and Lorraine, as well as some parts of Burgundy. It was with one of these travelling lacemen that Claude Lorraine, the painter, first visited Italy in his boyhood.

Catherine de Medici set the fashion for lace in Paris. She brought from Florence in her suite Frederic Vinciolo, who was appointed pattern-maker for laces and needlework to the Court. He published a number of pattern-books at Paris, mostly for needle-point and darned net, but that of 1623 is said to have contained eight pillow patterns. Séguin's criticism is that Vinciolo shows an ignorance of technical detail; consequently his patterns are not well contrived.

During the reign of Henry III (1574–89) lace began to play a more important part in French fashions, especially as an edging to the frilled ruffs then in vogue. In the last years of Henry IV (1589-1610) ruffs gave place to turned-over collars of linen edged with lace. These, as we saw, de-manded a heavier style of trimming, and consequently the lace of this time is richer in character, becoming later on richer still, when the large linen collars were replaced by small turned-down collars, made entirely, or almost entirely, of lace.

The reign of Henry IV is the most prolific in French lace pattern-books. Most of the needle-point patterns of Vinciolo appeared at this time, but they do not concern our purpose. Séguin mentions what seems to be an important pattern-book, pub-lished at Montbelliard by Jacques Foillet in 1598. But with due respect to M. Séguin's authority, I feel

doubts as to the existence of this book. Only
one copy is mentioned, that of the "Bibliothèque
Nationale" in Paris, and this is said to have been
lost years ago. Foillet published in the same year
a collection of patterns for cutwork, and it may be
that the idea of the existence of a second collection
is due to some confusion.

In 1605, however, there is a well-authenticated
French pattern-book, or one might say Anglo-
French, that of the "très excellent Milour[1] Matthias
Mignerak, anglois ouvrier fort expert en toute sorte
de lingerie." It was edited and published by Jean
le Clerc at Paris under the title of " La Pratique de
l'Aiguille Industrieuse." For the most part it contains patterns for darned net, remarkable for their
methodical arrangement and strange subjects. The
author seems to have had in mind the construction of
some great coverlid in squares, some with scenes,
others with flower-pots or trees for variety. The
scenes are most ambitious, representing Danae with
the shower of gold, Lucretia piercing her breast,
the elements, the seasons, "la Charité Romaine,"
and other curious pictures. At the end of the book
he gives twelve patterns of "passements faicts au
Fuzeau," which is all that directly concerns us.
They are much in the style of Parasole, but show less
practical knowledge than do most of hers.

The pattern-book published by Vinciolo in 1623
falls in the next reign. Unfortunately no copy is
accessible to me. It seems to have been the last

[1] My lord.

French pillow-lace pattern-book published.[1] Ladies
had given up practising the art of pillow lace ; it
had already developed into styles more difficult for
an amateur to copy than the light easy patterns of
"Le Pompe" or even those of Parasole. They re-
verted to needle points, which needed no special
training nor tools, leaving pillow lace to professional
workers. These latter for the most part kept to two
or three patterns, at which they constantly worked,
a woman sometimes rearing a whole family on the
produce of a single pattern not an inch broad. So
though lace-making developed into a fine art, patterns
were less and less in demand.

From the time of Henry IV[2] lace, which had thus
far been used on body and house linen, came into
more general use, and soon was worn on everything
down to garters, shoes and boot tops, trimming equip-
ages, coffins, and even baths. But though this was
the case, the French lace trade does not seem to have
been very large, most of the commodity being imported. Cardinal Mazarin tried to suppress the
importation of foreign laces and improve the small
home manufacture by the purchase of patterns in
Italy and the Netherlands.[3] During the first half
of the seventeenth century many edicts were issued
with this intention. No laces were to be worn save
those made in the kingdom, and not above a certain
value per ell ; or laces were to be allowed only on the
collar and edge of the cloak, on the sleeve seams and
down the middle of the back, along the buttons

[1] Séguin, p. 51.   [2] Séguin, p. 35.   [3] Ilg, 49.

and button-holes, and at the edge of the basques of the doublet,[1] and so forth, with an infinity of detail. Mostly the idea is to prevent waste of money, and especially the squandering of it on foreign products ; but an ordonnance at Le Puy, in 1640, forbids lace on the ground of its obliterating class distinctions, since it was worn by all classes, and still more because of the "servant question," so many women making lace that it was impossible to obtain servants.

Mazarin's successor in office, Jean Baptiste Colbert, was not at all of the opinion of the parlement of Le Puy. Chief among the various industrial enterprises which he set on foot to revive the commerce and finance of the country was the lace trade.[2] Till then unimportant for the kingdom as a whole, it has ever since the time of Colbert been a real item in French commerce. We have seen that ten years before Colbert's coming into office[3] the industry played a great part already in the district of Le Puy ; and at the beginning of the seventeenth century Catherine de Rohan, Duchess of Longueville, had brought workers from Havre and Dieppe to Chantilly.[4] But Colbert introduced the lace trade into many new districts, first starting a school in the castle of Lonray, at Alençon,[5] the property of his daughter-in-law. This was followed by others at Quesnoy, Arras, Reims, Sedan, Château Thierry, Loudun, and Aurillac—some for point, some for pillow lace. He showed discernment

---

[1] Séguin, p. 57.
[2] His activity is well summed up in the "Edinburgh Review," 1872, p. 51 ff.
[3] He became King's Councillor in 1651.   [4] Ilg, p. 55.
[5] Alençon became a great centre for needlepoint.

in developing the pillow-lace industry especially in the towns of the Flemish frontier, which were already used to seeing the laces made by their Belgian neighbours.[1] Besides providing for the instruction of workers in the different towns by competent lace-makers, many of whom he had, with infinite pains and secrecy, brought from Venice through the agency of the French ambassador there, he started a central institution for the working out of new patterns at the Château de Madrid in Paris. This supplied models to all the other centres in France, and exercised a most happy influence on French taste. The years from the time of Colbert's coming into power until nearly the end of the reign form the most brilliant period in the evolution of lace. The patterns in use were extremely elaborate and closely woven, but neither clumsy nor clothy in effect, and the execution shows a sureness and mastery over all the infinity of bobbins required that leaves one puzzling how, with such primitive tools, it was ever possible to realize such complex and perfect tissues, rendering so many degrees of light and shade, of high and low relief.

The end of the reign of Louis XIV was, however, a time of general exhaustion, and the lace trade naturally suffered with the rest. The Château de Madrid ceased to supply patterns.[2] The impoverished nobles could no longer pay such heavy prices for the beautiful guipures, and lace took a new development. Designs covering the whole of a piece

[1] Cole, "Cantor Lectures," p. 9.   [2] Séguin, p. 68.

of lace were replaced by scattered *motifs*, and the space between them was filled by some soft light grounding (Fig. 18). Somewhat less time and a good deal less skill were needed in making these grounded laces. The fashion of the time demanded a lace that would frill; their texture was soft, and they draped gracefully in folds, which concealed the pattern, so that less attention was paid to boldness and beauty of design. These laces continued in fashion throughout the reign of Louis XV, and have ever since formed the greater proportion of French pillow laces—for instance, Chantilly, Lille, and the blonds of Bayeux. The Vosges, however, and Le Puy have retained older traditions—not those of Colbert, but of the early seventeenth-century guipures. For the beautiful guipures of the best period, such as those of Sedan, we look nowadays in vain. Indeed, it is most unlikely that any one in the future would be content to lavish skill, time, and eyesight in such extravagance on a few square inches of lace, even for the satisfaction of making it a world's wonder; and if one sometimes regrets the lost art, one is more than reconciled to the loss by the improved condition of the worker.

The following reign brought worse times for lace. To neglect in the matter of design had succeeded absolute indifference (Fig. 17). Marie Antoinette introduced the fashion of fichus of muslin or of the bobbin-net made at Tulle, and named after that town. These with their folds and frills replaced lace to a great extent. When lace was used to trim them, it was

FIG. 17. FRENCH LAPPET (LOUIS XVI)
FIG. 18. FRENCH LACE (LOUIS XV)

frilled on full, and any insignificant pattern served the purpose. The French Revolution was not likely to encourage the art; indeed, it is said that some lace-makers of Chantilly were guillotined because they had worked for the queen. Under the Directoire, the Consulate, and well into the First Empire, the classical fashion of dress prevented much use of lace except on underwear, and as this last was during that time in France of the slightest character, the lace trade continued to suffer. Napoleon, with character-istic grasp of detail, recognized its importance for the country and encouraged it by large purchases, and by making lace obligatory on Court dresses.[1] He himself chose the laces for Marie Louise's *corbeille de noce*, spending over 80,000 francs on them.

An event occurred in 1817 which proved of the greatest importance for the lace trade in France, but whether for good or evil it is difficult to say. Machines for the manufacture of "bobbin-net" were smuggled from England to Lyons, and henceforward the hand-made groundwork of the time of Louis XV was frequently supplanted by net, on to which separate hand-made *motifs* were sewed. This combination can never be anything but a cheap substitute; the texture of machine net cannot compare with the gloss and soft elasticity of pillow-made grounds. Machine-made nets were also sprigged and run by hand in the fashion of Limerick lace; such French work is nowadays called *dentelle bretonne*. Twenty years later the Jacquard looms brought in the first pos-

[1] A. Lefébure, p. 34.

sibilities of regular machine-made lace. This in
France, as everywhere else, has damaged the interests
of the handworker, an uncultivated eye not grasping
the differences in the two fabrics. Indeed, with
modern improvements in lace machines it has become
difficult sometimes even for a trained eye to do so.
But after all there is no need to despair of the old
handicraft. Séguin[1] most happily explains one of
the reasons why machine-made lace cannot equal
the hand work that it imitates : "In machine work
the operating force is uniform, continually the same,
hence there is always an equal tension in the threads
and a perfectly regular tissue is produced, but at the
same time perfectly flat. Hand work, on the contrary,
is bound to be irregular, because, though the worker's
hand represents a forcé of a uniform strength, its
action is unequal and cannot be regulated in the
same way as can a mechanical force." He goes
on to point out the advantage of this irregularity
by alluding to the uneven surface of hand-woven
cashmere shawls "presenting an infinite succession
of waves and little imperceptible roughnesses, which
catch the light and cast shadows," making a surface
vastly different from anything a machine can produce ; different in somewhat the same way in which
the inside of a limpet shell differs from that of a
"sea-ear." The one is flat, dead white ; the other
by its irregularities breaks the light into the prismatic
colours we call mother-o'-pearl, and these colours

[1] p. 93.

depend only on the uneven surface of the shell ; a cast taken in sealing-wax will reproduce them.

It must also be remembered that the best flax thread is too soft to bear the tension needed by a machine, hence the " poor " texture of machine laces whose thread has perforce been adulterated with cotton in order to make it more resisting.

Besides, it will always be costly to vary patterns on lace machines frequently, and taste will never tolerate wholesale consumption of a single pattern in trimmings. As soon as a collar is widely known it ceases to please, so that even if machine laces were far more generally successful in imitation than they are, the art of lace-making is not likely to fall into disuse.

Some help is being afforded to the industry in France by legislation,[1] and a good deal more by the enterprise of different lace firms, the heads of which have contrived to interest the public by lectures and the publication of books.[2] It is doubtless owing to the intelligent guidance and good taste of such men that France preserves so high a reputation for her laces.

Her chief district for fine pillow laces at the present day is Normandy, whither the old Chantilly industry has been transferred, owing to the increasing cost of living round Paris.[3] Caen and Bayeux are the two centres, and a great deal of silk blond and black silk

[1] A. Lefébure, 93 ff.
[2] The works so frequently cited here, by J. Séguin, A. Lefébure, and E. Lefébure, are instances.   [3] Bury Palliser, p. 215.

lace is made. Of Valenciennes we have spoken in considering Belgium, for that lace is made in far greater quantity across the frontier. Lille, I believe, still produces fine narrow lace *à réseau*. More important by far is the Vosges district, with Mirecourt as head-quarters of the trade. A variety of guipures, some copies of sixteenth and seventeenth century models, some modern and elaborate, are made here. Le Puy also produces a great quantity of admirable coarse guipures (Fig. 19).

THE SPANISH LACE TRADE is and always has been of far less consequence than one would expect. Spain has published no lace pattern-books.[1] The general theory is that she learned lace-making from Flanders, but at what period is disputed. Riaño doubts the existence of a native industry before the eighteenth century,[2] Spain up to that time depending for the commodity, which was in great demand, on imports from Flanders and France. Mrs. Bury Palliser, however, states that pillow lace was made in La Mancha and Catalonia before 1665,[3] and A. S. Cole that the lace trade of Barcelona was worked up after Flemish models toward the end of the seventeenth century.[4] This earlier dating is supported by the mention of Spanish "gueuse" (a kind of coarse guipure, or according to others Torchon) in the often quoted satirical French poem of the "Révolte des Passements" published at the time of the sumptuary edict of 1660. That these old Spanish laces were coarse and of no

---

[1] Cole, "Cantor Lectures," p. 25.   [2] Riaño, p. 275.
[3] Bury Palliser, p. 44.   [4] "Cantor Lectures," p. 8.

distinction is seen also from the testimony of a
Spanish author, quoted by Riaño, who, writing in
1775, says: "Lace is employed to a very considerable extent; all the fine qualities come from foreign
lands, and the greater varieties of the coarse ones.
Spanish matrons, among other branches of their
education, are taught to make lace of different kinds,
and many respectable people live on this industry."
The districts in which pillow lace was then made were
Madrid, Barcelona, La Mancha, Almagro, Zamora,
Granatula, and Manzanares; and there was quite a
lively industry both in thread, silk, and gold laces.
Coarse thread laces are to this day a staple of trade
at Barcelona and in Catalonia, as also are silk blonds.
Gold and silver lace is made at Barcelona, Talavera
de la Reyna, Valencia, and Seville.

As to PORTUGAL little information is obtainable.
At present pillow lace is made in and near Lisbon, at
Vianna do Castello, Setubal, and Faro in Algarve.[1]
The Portuguese seem to have had a hand in teaching
the art to several other peoples; Ceylon, Travancore,
and other Indian laces are said to have a Portuguese
character.[2]

MADEIRA must have learned from the governing
country, but the lace trade of the island does not
seem destined to flourish. It had died out in 1850,
when it was re-established by an English lady, and
managed later on to support seven families. It does
not take much to support the natives of Madeira. But
in 1901, in spite of diligent inquiry in Funchal, I

[1] Bury Palliser, p. 106.   [2] *Ibid.*, p. 88.

could find no trace of any such work beyond Swiss embroidery and a little drawn thread.

A more creditable pupil of Portugal is BRAZIL. Here again there is no information accessible, but the Victoria and Albert Museum has a number of Brazilian specimens of what may perhaps best be called Torchons, but that have a charm and character quite beyond what one is accustomed to connect with that class of lace. The ground is Torchon, but the figures are varied and well chosen, the workmanship excellent.

ENGLAND has two principal lace-making districts; Devon is one, and a part of the South Midlands, including Northampton, Bedford, and Buckingham, the other. Each has a distinct character; the Devonshire lace (Honiton) resembling Flemish guipure, such as Brussels (Fig. 22), while the older[1] Midland patterns have a mixed character, Flemish of the Antwerp and Mechlin kinds on the one hand, and French (Lille and Norman) on the other. They are always grounded, never guipure (Figs. 20, 21). And these characteristics have their origin in history, for Devon learnt early from Flemish refugees from Alva's persecution, learning apparently once and for all; there is no record of the little community that brought the art, nor of any subsequent arrivals. The older guipure lace was mastered and retained. In the Midlands, on the other hand, we have evidence of many successive arrivals of Flemings, later of French Huguenots, and last of French *émigrés* from

---

[1] After the 1851 Exhibition these patterns gave way to Maltese.

FIG. 19. LE PUY LACE (MODERN)
FIG. 20. BUCKINGHAMSHIRE LACE (MODERN)
FIG. 21. NORTHAMPTONSHIRE LACE (MODERN)

FIG. 22. HONITON LAPPET (FIRST HALF NINETEENTH CENTURY)

the Revolution. The Midlands then had opportunity to learn the later forms of grounded laces, and these it was that came to stay. The Flemish origin of many of these laces is shown not only by the patterns, but by Flemish terms the lace-makers use, such as "trolly" for gimp.

We hear of "bone lace" in England as early as 1554, when Sir Thomas Wyatt went to his execution in a ruff trimmed with it.[1] But we do not seem to have distinguished ourselves in pattern-making, except in as far as we may lay claim to the "très excellent Milour Matthias Mignerak anglois."[2] Despite le Clerc's testimony to his nationality, his outlandish name makes one sceptical of English parentage. Another who, like Mignerak, has a name more Flemish than English is Richard Shorleyker; but at least his book is printed "in Shoelane at the signe of the Faulcon 1632," and with a good English title, "A Scholehouse for the Needle." His patterns closely resemble those of Mignerak, but not having been able to compare them directly one with the other,[3] I cannot definitely state what I more than suspect—that he republishes the older patterns. An earlier book (1596) of "curious and strange Inventions," published "for the profit and delight of the Gentlewomen of England," by William Barley, contains no pillow-lace patterns, and is on its own confession reprinted from a Venetian pattern-book.

During the sixteenth and seventeenth centuries

---

[1] A. M. S., p. 172. [2] See above, p. 38.
[3] Mignerak is in the British Museum, Shorleyker at South Kensington.

both area and importance of the English lace trade were considerably greater than they are now. The Midland district included Cambridge, Hertford, and Oxford, joining by Wiltshire the southern one, which stretched from Hampshire to Cornwall.[1] In 1698 a petition to Parliament calls the "lace manufacture in England the greatest next to the woollen," and estimates the number of workers earning a living by it at one hundred thousand.[2] Earlier is Thomas Fuller's testimony, and so charmingly worded that it must be quoted in full, as it stands in his "Worthies" under Devonshire's manufactures.[3]

"Bonelace. Much of this is made in and about Honyton, and weekly returned to London. Some will have it called Lace, *à Lacinia*, used as a fringe, on the borders of cloaths; *Bone-lace* it is named, because first made with *bone* (since *wooden*) *bobbins*. Thus it is usual for such utensills both in the Latine and English Names, gratefully to retain the memory of the first matter they were made of; as *Cochleare*, a *Spoon*, (whether made of Wood or Metal) because Cockle-shells were first used to that purpose.

"Modern is the use thereof in *England*, not exceeding the middle of the Raign of Queen *Elizabeth*: Let it not be condemned for a superfluous wearing, because it doth neither hide nor heat, seeing it doth adorn: Besides, (though private persons pay for it) it stands the State in nothing, not expensive of Bullion, like other Lace, costing nothing save a little thread descanted on by art and industry: Hereby many

---

[1] Bury Palliser, p. 371.	[2] *Ibid.*, p. 402.
[3] Ed. 1662, p. 246.

children, who otherwise would be burthensome to
the Parish, prove beneficial to their Parents : Yea,
many lame in their limbs, and impotent in their arms,
if able in their fingers, gain a lively-hood thereby ;
Not to say, that it saveth some thousands of pounds
yearly, formerly sent over Seas, to fetch Lace from
Flanders."

Save to England some thousands of pounds yearly
it very well might, considering the prices paid in
the late seventeenth and early eighteenth centuries.
Dorset and Devon lace fetched £6 per yard, and lest
it be assumed that this was specially wide, we may
add that a narrow piece of Lyme Regis lace, enough
to set on plain round an old woman's cap, was valued
at four guineas.[1] Defoe speaks of the exquisitely fine
lace of Blandford, rated above £30 sterling a yard.
£15 was paid for an 18-inch square of plain bobbin
net made at Honiton.   It must be remembered that
the fine thread needed was also excessively dear ; in
1790 it was brought from Antwerp at £70 the pound.
Still there was a handsome margin for profit, and it is
no wonder that the trade spread.   Ripon and Suffolk
produced lace, and in 1775 an attempt was made
under the patronage of Queen Charlotte to teach
poor London children, but without lasting effect.

In England, as indeed everywhere else, a marked
decline in the lace industry began from about 1780
onwards. This is partly accounted for by the pseudo-
classical fashions in dress, which then prevailed all
over Europe, partly by the burden wars had laid on

[1] Bury Palliser, p. 398.

the country, and also by the increasing use of machine-made trimmings and of muslins. From the time of Queen Adelaide royal patronage was secured to Honiton lace, but the industry languished until for a while it was galvanized into life by the Great Exhibition of 1851. This impetus was counteracted by the perfecting of lace machines, and it is not likely that pillow lace will ever again recapture the second place among British industries.

Of late years, however, fashion has brought lace into great prominence, and the increased demand has caused revivals of various local industries. Winchelsea, for instance, where lace had long been forgotten, now owns a school with a score of pupils ; and among other patterns, a rough design of hops, supposed to have originated in the place itself, is made once more. Suffolk has again taken to lace-making. The Midlands, where since the time of the 1851 Exhibition quantities of cotton lace of Maltese pattern had been produced, now provide a much greater variety of styles (Fig. 23).

Even more encouraging is the improvement in design noticeable in Honiton laces, due to the initiative of several ladies who have lace schools, or have interested themselves in making new patterns or adapting old Italian ones. Honiton lace has always deserved its reputation for workmanship, but its patterns had till lately been going from bad to worse, formed as they were of naturalistic flowers and insects, without any attempt at continuity of design, and very little at broad effect, for which there is so

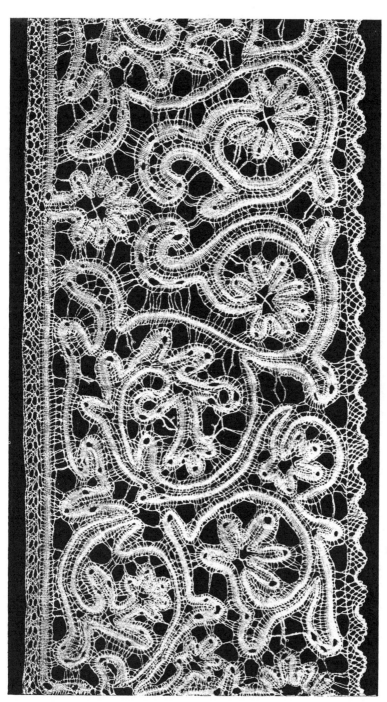

FIG. 23. MODERN "RUSSIAN" LACE (MADE AT THE WINSLOW LACE SCHOOL)

much scope in the well-known Honiton bridal veils and state dresses.

A. S. Cole, in a parliamentary report on Honiton lace (1888, vol. LXXX), quite accounts for the ugliness of these patterns. A lace-worker at Beer told him how they were designed. "Sometimes we see a new wall-paper and prick a pattern off it, changing a bit here, or leave a little or add a little." Another adapted her patterns from "wall-papers, tablecloths, or anything." The sprigs thus devised out of cottage wall-papers were made separately, and sold to some other worker to join together in one confused mosaic. If patterns of a different character were chosen, "the gentlefolks called it machine."

In IRELAND pillow lace is a negligible quantity compared with the allied arts of point lace, crochet, and various forms of linen embroidery. There seems to be a small peasant industry at Carrickfergus in narrow pillow laces, and some of the convents, among them the one at Parsonstown, copy Honiton patterns.[1]

SCOTLAND[2] has never dealt much in lace, though several attempts have been made to introduce the industry. One was at Edinburgh in the middle of the eighteenth century by the Duchess of Hamilton, one of the beautiful Miss Gunnings. A quarter of a century later a woman from Lille taught lace-making in Glasgow and Renfrew. Neither of these industries seems to have survived, but better fortune

[1] Cole, "Dublin Lectures," II, p. 19, and Bury Palliser, p. 446.
[2] Bury Palliser, p. 428.

attended one at New Pitsligo, Aberdeenshire,[1] where, soon after 1820, a cobbler's wife from Huntly began lace-making, and, the clergyman and laird interesting themselves in the matter, the village took it up. Thirty or forty workers are still employed, some on quite elaborate patterns.

Before we leave the subject of British laces, we must mention the influence of missionaries in teaching our patterns to Indians, Chinese, and, I believe, to the Malagasy. The India and China Museum at South Kensington has a collection of Indian laces, which for the most part plainly speak to the influence of the Midland patterns, both the older French and Flemish kinds and the modern Maltese. From the labels of the collection, it is evident that the lace industry is not confined to the missionary schools, but has spread among the ladies of Bombay and other towns. The thread laces show little or no originality, but the gold and silver lace seems to bear marks of being a true native product.

About the age of the RUSSIAN lace industry opinions differ. Its origin has been traced[2] to Peter the Great, who was said to have introduced it to Novgorod from France, but this, on the face of it, is false. It is characteristic of French laces that they none of them employ *crochetage*, and equally characteristic of Russian ones that they nearly always do so. Peter, if he introduced the industry, must have chosen Flemish workers, for Russian lace is most akin to the

---

[1] Article in the " Weekly Scotsman " of 2 September, 1905.
[2] Bury Palliser, p. 283.

guipures of Flanders and Brabant. There is indeed a tradition to the effect that in 1725 he brought lace-makers from various convents in Brabant to the convent of Novodevitschy to teach lace-making and spinning.

It is difficult to determine whether or no it is patriotism that prompts Madame Davydoff to set the origin of Russian lace back into the Middle Ages. Slavs as a rule make better patriots than pedants, and there are many well-known cases where they have let their national feeling run away with them to the extent of inventing all kinds of past achievements for their ancestors. This fact on the one hand, and the far more recent origin of lace in all the other European countries on the other, makes one hesitate to accept all the historical statements in the introduction to Madame Davydoff's most valuable work. Were one not told the contrary, one would say that these medieval specimens were simple eighteenth-century patterns. But, of course, if the vestments they trim are intact and of proven antiquity, there is no more to be said against this early dating. The quotations from old documents which the author gives to prove the existence of lace at certain dates, are constantly open to the objection that we are not sure what meaning their terms conveyed to contemporaries. Certainly this is difficult ground.

Great quantities of lace, mostly of coarse thread in vermiculated patterns, are produced in Central Russia; 32,514 lace-makers are employed. The chief districts for it are Belev, Vologda, Riazan, and

Mzensk, and there is a new school of lace under imperial patronage at Moscow. A good idea of the possibilities of Russian lace was given by an exhibition in London (autumn, 1904), organized by the Zemstvo of the Vologda district. A great variety was shown, some extremely beautiful, both in design and execution. There were large scarves and bed-covers and most curious combinations of colours, beside the ordinary Russian laces, of which the examples in chapter VII give a fair idea. All the more elaborate pieces were of the mazy kind; the simpler patterns included grounded laces, whose geometrical design was formed by gimps, and many Torchons. Beside these laces a good deal of gold and silver lace is made. Odessa, though not itself manufacturing laces, does a considerable trade in them in open market.

FINLAND has a lace industry at Nardendal, near Abo.

In SWEDEN the peasants of Dalecarlia make lace for their own consumption. The only trade centre for lace is Wadstena, where it was long a convent industry. Of late years some charming eighteenth-century patterns have been revived.

CRETAN laces are well represented in the India and China Museum. They have a barbaric air, from the many-coloured threads and the curious clumsy figures of men, birds, and animals worked in them.

Having then considered in brief the past history and present geography of pillow lace, we will pass to the practical side of the subject.

CHAPTER III

TOOLS

Puis qu'ainsi t'est predestiné, voudrois tu faire espoincter les fuseaulx, calumnier les bobines, reprocher les devidoirs, condemner les pelotons des Parques?—Rabelais, "Pantagruel," Book III.

THE tools required for making pillow lace present no great hindrance to the intending worker, either for their number or cost. With exception of the bobbins and the winder, they are either articles in daily use or such as can easily be made by the worker herself. She may dispense with the winder at a pinch, and the bobbins are easily turned by any one who can work a lathe; so that the length of this chapter need not discourage the beginner. I have described different forms of pillow, etc., at some length, not because I think the worker is bound to provide herself with several kinds, but so that if one does not suit her she can try another. For not only do these different forms adapt themselves more easily, some to one kind of lace, some to another; even more than this, there are the personal ways of the worker to take into account. It does not come naturally to every one to work in one and the same way, and slight differences in method may make one kind of pillow far more comfortable in use than another. The short-sighted worker will use a different stand from that which suits her long-sighted sister.

And here I should like to protest against the hide-bound conservatism that rules—sad to say—especially in women's handicrafts. Why should we so illiberally cling to some traditional way of holding the hands in our work as the only correct one? Why cannot we recognize the fact that our hands are shaped differently, the strength of our muscles balanced differently, that some are stronger in the wrist, some in the fingers, and so can never use their force to best advantage by all trying to pose themselves in some one accepted traditional way?

In many parts it is traditionally correct to hold a great number of bobbins in the hands while working. It *is* possible in this way for some to economize the time they would spend in taking up and setting down the pairs in use. But that is no reason why the beginner should feel herself clumsy and amateurish because she can work better with only two pair in hand at a time. This is much less confusing, and I have known a fairly experienced worker to waste more than the time she gained in having the bobbins so close at hand, by being obliged to undo a good part of her work because she had got hold of the wrong pairs. The Flemish lacemakers, who work very fast indeed, retain no bobbins in the hands, but let them all lie in a row on a stiff card fastened across the pillow, lifting each bobbin in turn over the next.

Work in the way that comes natural to you. There

is no need to follow slavishly the rules laid down in this or in any other book, in order to become expert. If the instructions given here appear precise and dogmatic, it is because to give a choice of methods confuses and worries the beginner, not that only one road "leads to Rome." Later on, the worker, gaining experience, will find short cuts and ways of her own.

Take pains to find the most comfortable pose for working, the best heights for table, stand, and chair, so that you do not have to bend over your work, nor fatigue your arms with raising them unduly. These details, unnoticed at first through absorption in the work, afterwards make themselves most unpleasantly apparent in stiff neck or arms.

Do not hurry because you have heard professional workers clicking their bobbins at a great rate; remember that they mostly make one pattern day after day. The amateur has no need to turn herself into a machine, and cannot expect to work as fast as if she did so. Lace-making is a pleasant and soothing employment; if it "excites the nerves," as I have heard German ladies complain, it is because the worker does not take it in the right spirit, either regarding it as a task to be finished quickly, or as an opportunity of "showing off."

But to return to our tools. Chief among them is the PILLOW. Whatever the size or shape, it must be stuffed hard and evenly, and its different covers must not be so thick or closely woven as to offer resistance to the pins. The outer cover should be

washable and of some colour restful to the eye, preferably without a pattern, as this tends to dazzle the
worker.

1. A cylindrical pillow is best for yard-work.[1] It
is convenient to have it of a definite girth, as this
enables the worker to calculate the length of lace
made without continual measurement; 18 in. is a
good size. If the pillow is made much larger, it is
cumbersome, especially for taking away from home;
if it is smaller, the join in the pattern (and it is sometimes difficult to effect this invisibly) comes round
all the oftener. As to length, it must be long enough
to take the widest laces with a margin of 3 in. or so
on each side for the long pins, on which the bobbins
not at the moment in use are hung out of the way.
That will be about 10 in. (Fig. 33).

Cut a strip of Hessian (or any strong stuff not too
close in texture, so as readily to admit the pins) 18 in.
by 15 in. (turnings not allowed). Hem both long
sides so as to admit a strong tape runner; join the
shorter sides by a seam. Cut two circles of stout
card with a radius of $2\frac{3}{4}$ in.[2]

Set tapes in the runner hems : draw one up tight
and knot it, leaving the other open. This forms a
bag ; cover the hole left by the gathering at the
bottom with one of the cards.

The next business is the stuffing, for which differ-

---

[1] Lengths of edging or insertion as distinguished from shaped pieces of
lace.

[2] These will, of course, be slightly under the 18 in. in circumference, but the
thickness of the coverings and the stretching caused by tight stuffing should
make the finished pillow practically accurate.

ent materials may be used. Hay with stones makes a very fair stuffing ; the stones should be laid in the middle out of the way of the pins ; they are needed to give the pillow weight, otherwise the bobbins constantly drag it round. Bran or sawdust mixed with silversand is another good stuffing, easier to make even. Emery would answer all requirements, being not only heavy, but saving steel pins from rust, which is the great curse with hay pillows, for it not only spoils the pins, but sometimes stains the lace with iron-mould. Emery by itself, however, is too heavy except for a very small pillow, but an empty cylindrical cocoa-tin set in the middle of the pillow would bring it down to a more reasonable weight. Whatever your material, stuff the pillow as tightly as possible, lay the second card circle in the open mouth of the bag and draw up the runner, tying it very tightly. This finishes the pillow.

The outer cover is cut like the inner one, save that it should measure 20 in. by 14 in., and the shorter sides should have two narrow hems added instead of the seam. These will be fastened one over the other on the cushion with pins. The ends are drawn up with ribbons, and small card circles, covered with material of some contrasting colour, are slipped inside to make all neat. The pillow is then ready for use. Honiton workers generally use a number of small movable cover-cloths to keep the lace clean. I have never found them necessary, and they are a complication, but, especially in towns, it is well to have some large handkerchief, or embroidered cloth, to throw over the pillow if it is left to stand out in the room.

This shape of pillow requires a STAND to complete it. Saxon workers often use a cardboard box about 3 in. deep, the same length as the pillow, but not quite so wide. It is a simple expedient, but not ideal, being untidy, soon worn out, and, what is worse, unless the table at which the worker sits is particularly high, such a stand does not raise the pillow near enough to the eyes, and to bend the head over lacework very soon incapacitates the worker with a stiff neck. A shallow basket or wooden tray is open to the same objection.

Wooden stands are better. I have seen three kinds almost equally good : A (shown in Fig. 33) raised the pillow well ; B (Fig. 29) might be mounted on a box to hold thread, scissors, and extra bobbins. The most portable form, and one which cannot possibly be broken, is simply a rectangular block of wood with the top hollowed lengthways to hold the cylindrical pillow.

2. Another cylindrical pillow (Fig. 26)[1] most frequent in France would not be so easily made at home, since it requires some carpentry. Its foundation is a board about 18 in. square. Slightly to the rear of the centre is set a lidless wooden box about 5 in. by 8 in. and 5 in. deep. Flock is set all round the box and sloped gradually down to the level of the board as it reaches the edge. This flock, when

---

[1] Our illustration is from a pillow kindly lent by Messrs. Ponting Bros., High Street, Kensington.

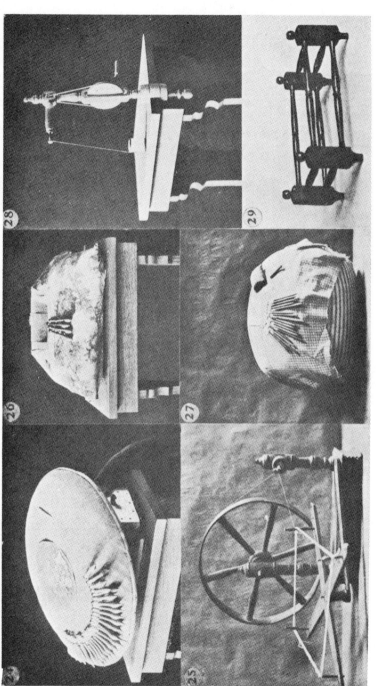

FIG. 24. BELGIAN LACE PILLOW
FIG. 25. OLD ENGLISH LACE TURN

FIG. 26. FRENCH PILLOW
FIG. 27. HONITON PILLOW

FIG. 28. GERMAN WINDER
FIG. 29. STAND FOR CYLINDRICAL PILLOW

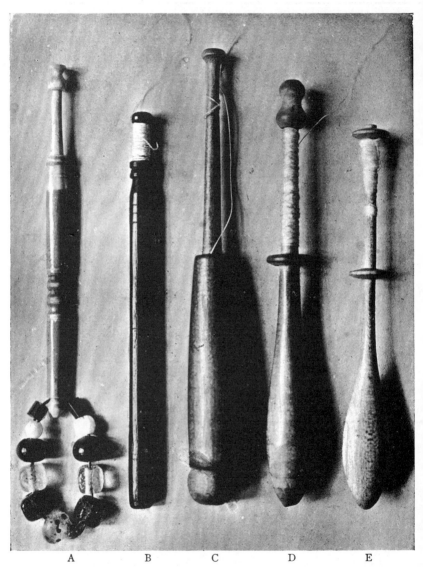

FIG. 30   BOBBINS (natural size)

tightly covered, forms a sort of desk, sloping from the box (which is to contain a cylindrical pillow), and on this the bobbins rest when not in use. In the middle of one shorter side of the box is a hole, of the other, a groove, to receive the axle of the pillow. A ratchet engaging a wheel on the axle prevents the cylinder from slipping round. The pillow is a wooden reel, with an axle which projects at each end fitting into the hole and groove in the box. It is wound round tightly and evenly, first with tow, then with a few layers of flannel, till the waist of the reel is brought flush with its circular ends.

3. Another form of pillow for yard-work is the Belgian lace desk. Being made in two parts, the worker, starting from the top of the smaller piece, can work down to the bottom of the larger and then fit the small piece into the bottom of the large one, replacing it later at the top.

None of these pillows are suitable for shaped pieces.

4. For these the Belgians use a mushroom-shaped disc (Fig. 24)[1] made of a circular piece of board, padded. It revolves on a pivot set in the sloping top of a box containing a drawer for the bobbins.

5. Devonshire lace-makers use a great ball (Fig. 27) made of flock swathed round and round with list till it is 36 in. to 38 in. in circumference. The top is flattened, and padded with layers of flannel. The cover is made of a circle of twill, the same size as the

[1] Kindly lent by Messrs. Ponting Bros.

top of the pillow, and seamed on to this circle, a straight piece deep enough to cover the sides and almost meet beneath the pillow. The straight part is finished with a broad hem, through which a strong runner is passed to fasten the cover. Our illustration is from a pillow in the Victoria and Albert Museum, South Kensington.

6. But the amateur making her own pillow for shaped pieces will find it easiest to seam together two circles about 18 in. in diameter, of strong soft material, leaving 4 in. or 5 in. open for stuffing. Stuff it hard with bran and sand, so that the centre is the thickest part, and close the seam. Such a pillow is shown in Fig. 37. Flat, square, or oblong mattress pillows are also in use. They are more troublesome to make than circular ones, and offer no special advantage.

Next in importance to the pillow come the BOBBINS (Fig. 30). These are turned out of wood, though there are ornamental ones of bone and ivory. B is one of the common English shapes, which perhaps it may be more convenient for the worker to adopt, for she will need a large number, and may have difficulty in obtaining other kinds. D and E are also nowadays easily obtained in London ; they are the kinds most used in Belgium and France. Both cost about 1s. per dozen. Cleaner and more comfortable in use are the German bobbins (C) with covers to protect the thread ; they cost 10 pfennige per pair. Cleaner still are the "fuseaux Cottier" —a French patent bobbin with a hollow handle, which unscrews to receive a little ball of thread. The end of the thread is brought out through a hole and fastened round the bobbin-head in the usual way. Another French patent kind is the "Tjevoli" : the head takes off, the thread is wound in little hollow rolls, which are slipped on to the stem of the bobbin, and the head replaced. These two systems, while they save the trouble of winding, have the disadvantage that the worker is limited to one make of thread, for of course special balls or rolls are needed for charging the bobbins. And the price is augmented, which is a consideration, for the worker who takes her lace seriously needs at least fifty pair of bobbins. A beginner, however, need not buy more than twenty pair for the start.

These are the chief types of bobbin, but there are all sorts of varieties. Some in use in the school of lace at Vienna have three-sided handles, and are weighted with lead to prevent their slipping out of place and causing entanglement. Old - fashioned English bobbins (A) from the Midlands are often trimmed with coloured glass beads called "jingles" ; the worker, looking at the handles (a bad practice, by the way), distinguished them by their colours. Others, of bone or ivory, are ornamented with designs traced by tiny holes drilled and coloured black or red. The owner's name is worked on them, or some inscription, "from J. B." or even —what had become of the fitness of things?— "Jesus wept!"

PINS are another great item. Indeed, as already

indicated, one authority on lace[1] goes so far as to connect the beginning of pillow lace with the comparative commonness of pins. There are traditions that before pins were much in use fishbones and splinters of bone took their place on the pillow; but certainly such tools would be a great hindrance.

English lace-makers' pins are slim brass pins, longer and sharper than toilet pins, but otherwise just like them. In Germany glass-headed steel pins are used. Both have their advantages: the English are cheaper, and do not rust; the German are much prettier, more comfortable to handle, and do not bend. If the latter are chosen two sizes are needed: thick pins about $1\frac{1}{2}$ in. long for the coarse lace, and fine ones for the fine. The larger size sometimes have brass stems, which avoids rust. Short hatpins are needed for keeping the bobbins arranged in groups.

The beginner is not bound to buy a BOBBIN-WINDER; but though not indispensable, it greatly lessens the drudgery of winding—a consideration when you are dealing with forty or fifty pair. Illustrations of two types of winder—German and English—are shown facing p. 62, the former (Fig. 28) lent by Messrs. Ponting Bros., the latter (Fig. 25) from an old "lace turn" in the Victoria and Albert Museum. Should a winder not be readily obtainable, a carpenter, even an amateur, could easily make one. The English and German models are both worked on the same principle: a large driving-wheel, turned by a handle, is connected by an elastic or string band with a

---

[1] A. S. Cole, "Lecture at Dublin on Lace-making," p. 9.

smaller wheel, which sets the bobbin spinning. The English winder, clumsy as are the examples I have seen, had an advantage in being provided with a spool-holder for the reel of thread in use ; but the German model is all the compacter for lacking this, and its place is easily supplied by making the reel revolve on a hatpin stuck into the pillow. Both models have the same defect: the clip which holds the bobbin in place is never strong enough to keep it steady as it whirls. The middle finger of the left hand must remedy this, while the thumb and first finger guide the thread.

The Belgian winder is nothing but a leather driving belt $\frac{1}{4}$ in. wide and a primitive arrangement of posts for holding the bobbin in place. The belt is held fast and tight by passing through a ring buttoned into the worker's bodice and over the bobbin. The worker, by pulling the belt constantly towards her, makes the bobbin revolve. The lidless box at the foot serves as stand and receptacle for bobbins.

Other special apparatus beyond pillow and stand, winder, bobbins, and pins, I have only found to be a needless and tiresome complication; but from time to time the worker will need a fine steel crochet-hook, and another crochet-hook whose point has been ground sharp like a pin, or else one of those whose hook can be unscrewed from the handle and an ordinary stout needle inserted in its place. A small pair of embroidery scissors and some needles complete the list of tools.

CHAPTER IV

PATTERNS

On dit improprement les beaux arts, car l'art est un ; l'idéal du beau en toute chose.—JOSEPH SÉGUIN.

THE most important accessory to a lace pillow is the pattern. Some Russian peasants are said to work without patterns, simply by counting the number of times they twist their threads,[1] but this could only be done with very simple laces. Many professionals work from patterns drawn on parchment in plain outline, with no indications for the pinholes ; and, indeed, with curved designs this liberty has great advantages, experience soon teaching the worker where to set her pins. This is especially the case with very fine laces. But the beginner is bound to follow conscientiously a detailed pattern, and moreover to keep a piece of the finished lace or a photograph of it near at hand, with which to compare her work until she knows the pattern by heart.

Beside the examples given in this book, there are easy Torchon patterns in Weldon's "Practical Torchon Lace," Myra's Library of Needlework (No. 30) "Pillow Lace," and the books on Torchon published by two firms of threadmakers, Messrs. Harris, of

[1] Davydoff, p. 9.

68

Cockermouth, and Barbour, of Lisburn. Other laces are given in No. 40 of "Needlecraft," published by the Manchester School of Embroidery, and in Weldon's "Pillow Lace" and "Honiton Lace."

To those who know German I can thoroughly recommend Sara Rasmussen's "Klöppelbuch" (Copenhagen, Andr. Fred. Höst & Sön, n. d.) and Frieda Lipperheide's "Das Spitzenklöppeln" (Berlin, 1898), both of which contain a variety of advanced patterns. Simpler, but also good, are Adele Voshage's "Das Spitzenklöppeln" (Leipzig, 1895), Tina Frauberger's "Handbuch der Spitzenkunde" (Seemann's Kunsthandbücher), Th. de Dillmont's "Encyclopedie der weiblichen Handarbeiten,"[1] "Das Klöppeln" in Ebhart's "Handarbeiten" (Berlin, Franz Ebhart). C. Braunmühl's "Das Kunstgewerbe in Frauenhand" (Berlin, 1885). If expense is no object, nothing could be better than the magnificent work of Carl Jamnig and Adelheid Richter, "Technik der geklöppelten Spitzen" (Vienna, 1886). For those who know French, there is "Les Dentelles aux fuseaux," published by "La Boule de Neige" at Le Mans; and there are excellent occasional articles on pillow lace in Hachette's weekly journals "La Mode Pratique" and "La Corbeille à Ouvrage."[2]

As all the patterns in the present work were taken from unpublished sources,[3] any of the books men-

---

[1] One of the excellent "D. M. C." pattern-books, published under the auspices of Dollfus Mieg & Co.

[2] The second is an abridged edition of the first.

[3] Except No. 43, reproduced by kind permission of Messrs. Hachette & Co., from "La Mode Pratique" of 1899.

tioned will bring fresh material to the worker. But she need not limit herself even to these patterns : the following methods of copying will place an endless variety at her disposal, and she will find that after having worked through one or two representative patterns of a type she will need no further explanations.

Should she have the means of PHOTOGRAPHY at hand, she can work with photographs made in the ordinary way from a negative, or (and this is cheaper and simpler) with prints taken direct from the lace on to blue paper. Photography is specially useful for enlarging or reducing patterns.

But there are three other mechanical methods of copying lace patterns—pricking, rubbing, and tracing.

1. PRICKING is the old traditional method, laborious, but giving the most durable result. It is only worth doing with a pattern that is to stand very hard wear. Leather-paper, card, and parchment are the most suitable materials for a pricked pattern ; if the first two are used, choose them tinted, so that they form a better background for the white threads. If the card is thin it can be afterwards strengthened by pasting thin canvas on the back of the pattern. The pattern to be copied should be pinned firmly on a cushion over the fresh piece of card, so that neither can slip out of place while the copy is being made. The lace-pillow or any other cushion will serve ; for long patterns I have sometimes found a sofa useful. A pin may be used for pricking, but it is much more convenient to use a tool with a handle,

and a bone-handled crochet-hook with a steel end answers the purpose excellently if the hook is ground to a point on the grindstone.[1] Stab your tool through each hole in the model, and so long as your cards do not slip you are bound to secure an accurate copy· Your pattern will be all the easier to follow, especially if it is complex, if when finished you touch in a few direction lines with a pen to mark its principal curves, etc.

2. RUBBING. If, however, instead of a bought pattern you wish to copy a piece of lace, take a drawing-board and pin out your model tightly and firmly. The best way to do this is with brass pins, which are knocked lightly into the wood and cut off almost flush with the lace by means of a pair of cutting pliers. Such fastenings come less in the way of rubbing than any others. If this is too much trouble, ordinary drawing-pins can be used ; they deface the rubbing, but the blank spaces they cause in the copy can afterwards be filled in by hand. Next take a sheet of foreign notepaper and pin it over the lace, setting your drawing-pins well outside the range of the pattern. Get a piece of heelball from any shoemaker ; hold it awhile in your closed hand till it is warm, then rub it lightly but firmly over the paper, always in one direction at a time, for rubbing to and fro tears the paper away from its pins and so ruins the copy. A little practice will show which direction secures the best copy ; of course it varies with the curves of the pattern. Experiment also shows the

[1] See p. 67.

kind of paper to receive the best impression. As a rule, bank-note is preferable, but for very fine laces thin Japanese or tissue-paper may be used, and sometimes thin whitey-brown packing paper best meets the case. The rubbing thus taken will give a complete copy of the lace. Blurred spots can afterwards be rectified with a pen, and the whole emphasized if needful. Indeed, it is better in any case to go over the chief direction lines with pen and ink before pinning the pattern to your pillow. The paper may be tinted with water-colour paint—it spares the eyesight when white thread is used for the lace. Mix your colour first in fair quantity and very wet. Place the pattern on a slanted drawing-board, and, beginning at the top, cover the whole design with colour, never letting the brush pass twice over the same piece of paper. This will secure an even, unsmeared surface of colour.

This method can also be used in copying a pricked card pattern ; if the rubbing be taken from the back, the pin-holes will be clearly marked on the paper. It is a quick and easy way of copying.

The paper pattern may be mounted on calico to strengthen it, but even that hardly makes it very durable, as the curved position in which it lies on the lace pillow and the constant pricking of the pins soon peel it off again. Unless tissue-paper has been used, a rubbing will always serve *once* as a pattern. If it has to serve over and over again, it had better be recopied by the following process.

3. TRACING. If you wish to copy a pattern from

a printed book, a rubbing, or a photograph, take a tracing in the usual way, but instead of paper use architect's tracing-cloth. This can be bought at 1s. 6d. the yard in very wide width, so that a yard makes any number of lace patterns. It is most convenient stuff to use. As transparent as tracing-paper, it cuts easily, but will not tear, takes up far less room in storing than the awkward rolls of card patterns, is very durable, and, though white or bluish, does not need tinting, since the colour of the pillow shows through it quite strongly enough to contrast with the white thread, and so spare the worker's eyesight. In fact, it is so eminently suitable that I cannot understand why I have never seen it in use. Trace on the unglazed side of the cloth, and use ink, as pencil rubs off and spoils the thread.

Tracing-cloth lends itself to another process, very useful in cases where in a printed book only one "repeat" of a length pattern is given. Cut a strip of the cloth long enough to go round your pillow. Trace the "repeat" at one end of the strip, then fold it backwards and forwards so that the whole length is divided into a number of folds, each exactly the size of the "repeat" and each vertically beneath it. Take the greatest care that the crease of each fold reaches *exactly* as far as the end of the "repeat," and does not project beyond it. Then pressing the folded cloth on to the pillow, stab each pinhole of the pattern through all the folds with a pricker. This is a very quick and convenient way with length patterns.

4. DRAWING. Rubbing does not damage lace, but

you may wish to copy some specimen in a museum or a private collection that you will not be allowed to rub ; or you may have a piece to copy that is badly worked or washed out of shape. In these cases you will have to draw your pattern, and beside compass, parallel rule, and protractor, will find squared paper to be of the greatest assistance. It can be bought at any stationer's. It is especially useful in the copying of simple Torchons ; indeed, one hardly needs a pattern for them if this paper is used, cut in crossway strips, so that the squares lie diamond-fashion ; the worker can then set her pins by count. Squared papers of different grades enlarge and decrease patterns almost automatically.

Pattern designing. Squared paper is equally useful in pattern designing. But this is by no means a simple matter ; the inexperienced worker will find that the bobbins constantly work themselves into awkward positions, so that there are here too many and there too few to support the fabric. Strictly geometrical Torchons are not hard to design, there being a few given stitches which must be used for the most part in diagonal lines. The limits that make such patterns easy to handle prescribe their interest.

It is more amusing to adapt a Torchon length-pattern to suit a round d'oyley. No definite rule can be given for such adaptation, but on the whole one can rely on compasses and ruler to carry one through the difficulties of a simple Torchon pattern. Two concentric circles—one for the outer, one for the inner edge of the lace, the outer divided evenly into spaces answering to the scallops of the model—and besides them the radii touching each of these divisions, give your principal construction lines. The circles correspond to the horizontal, the radii to the vertical lines of the model. We give an example in No. 38, adapted from No. 37 by the method described.

It is not difficult to design Russian laces, because one can see at a glance on the paper whether the curves touch one another often enough to make a firm fabric, and this is the one essential point in their construction. Other laces demand more practical experience.

I must, however, mention one other mechanical aid to design applicable to all classes. Corners can be evolved from the length patterns for laces and insertions by help of a piece of looking-glass (the thinner the better) with a straight edge. Set this across your pattern at an angle of forty-five degrees with the straight edge, moving it to and fro until it seems to you to reflect the prettiest corner. Draw a line along the edge of the glass a b, and another line c b meeting it at the straight edge of the lace and forming a right angle with the latter. Make a fresh tracing of the space enclosed between these lines. Fold the tracing cloth accurately along the line a b, and prick through both folds all the pinholes of the pattern. This gives you the new corner. Its only disadvantage is that in most cases it is necessary to add several pair of bobbins towards b, which are cut away again once the corner is turned. Specially designed corners do not always necessitate this addition, which weakens the fabric. The example we give needs no extra bobbins; it is formed from lace No. 15. Fig. 31 shows the lace with the piece of looking-glass placed across it in the position indicated by the dotted line a b in the diagram. Fig. 32 is the diagram of the resulting corner; a comparison with the pattern of No. 15, p. 129, will show the very slight alterations that were required.

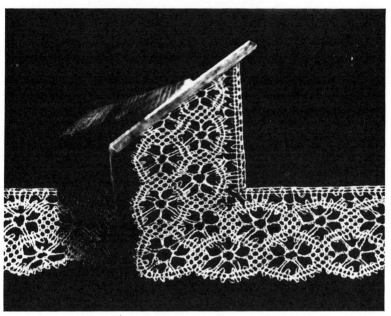

FIG. 31. PLANNING A CORNER WITH MIRROR

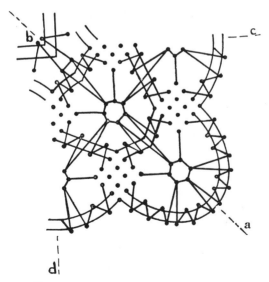

FIG. 32. PATTERN OF RESULTING CORNER

CHAPTER V

THREAD

A little thread descanted on by art and industry.—THOMAS FULLER.

THE first thing to be decided after the pattern is chosen is the kind of thread to be used and its degree of fineness.

Pillow lace can be made with a variety of materials. The aloe fibre, which is knitted into such beautiful patterns in Madeira, would make very fine lace. In Italy the brims of straw hats are sometimes formed of pretty passementeries, woven on a pillow with straws of different degrees of thickness and glossiness. Trimmings of uniforms and liveries were formerly, even more often than now, made in the same way with gold and silver threads ; hence the nursery rhyme about the "captain all covered with lace." Horsehair and human hair have been made to serve their turn on a lace pillow. It is well known that in needle lace horsehair is valuable for padding and stiffening the raised work of rich and heavy points. On the pillow, however, hair is only used for a whim, except by wig makers. The foundations of some of the best wigs are bobbined out of hair, which is not only less conspicuous for such a purpose, but lighter and more supple than other threads. String lace can be used for window blinds, and I have heard of an ingenious lady making a new seat to an old cane chair of macramé thread in half-stitch. A coarse simple pattern worked in chenille, or chenille and mercerized cotton, would make a suitable edge to a woollen table cover. The best-known form of woollen lace is Yak; the white is used for trimming flannel petticoats and dressing-gowns; black figured on certain old-fashioned mantles; but as to the hideous brown varieties, heaven only knows what is the good of them. In point of fact both wool and chenille are not in themselves well adapted for lace, though some woollen articles may call for such trimming.

Nor is cotton much better for our purpose. It fluffs in working and in washing; it looks poor, lacking the suppleness and gloss of good linen thread, nor is it so durable. It is often used simply because it is cheap, but the difference in price would never make it worth while for the amateur to use the inferior material. Still, I should like to make an exception in favour of lustrines and mercerized cottons. When a fast dye is chosen, they can be used effectively as a glossy outlining "gimp," in Torchon "fans," or in other cases where a colour is needed. Red ingrain cotton is another exception, having a faster dye than any coloured linen thread. It looks very well blended with white thread on coarse laces for towels and cloths that need constant washing.

Silk, whether black, white, or blond, is undeniably useful for working some light frail patterns, and as trimming for articles of dress that do not need frequent washing.

But none of the threads yet mentioned can be compared for general use with linen thread. It is the ideal material for lace, and but for the few exceptional cases already indicated, nothing else should be used. Supple, durable, sometimes glossy, sometimes of *mat* surface, but never dull, it lends itself to endless washing, and offers an infinite variety of thickness, from the thread fine as gossamer that snaps under any tension but the lightest, to the coarse gimp that shines like silk round the flowers it edges.

Never economize in thread, get the best. At the end of this book will be found a comparative table of the sizes of threads by some of the best-known makers. The sizes of linen thread do not, unfortunately, go by a uniform designation as do sewing cottons, and as it is of the greatest importance that the thread should be of the right size, this table will be of great use to the worker and spare her many tedious experiments. If too coarse a thread is used for the pattern chosen, the lace will be clumsy and clothy; if too fine it will be flimsy and poor. There is always a best size for each pattern, and very little deviation from it can be allowed. Black thread is sometimes used, unbleached also, and coloured flax thread, but for most purposes white is the best.

Having, then, chosen your thread, the next thing is to wind the bobbins.

To WIND BY HAND. Hold the bobbin (coverless) in your right hand, the head turned to your right. With your left hand place the end of thread towards you over the part of the bobbin furthest from the head. Cover it with your right thumb and wind away from you. You may, if you choose, wind in exactly the opposite direction, but whichever way you choose, *wind all your bobbins alike.* When the bobbin is full, if it has a cover, damp and straighten the end of the thread and drop it down the cover from the wide end, replacing the cover on the bobbin.

To prevent the thread unwinding itself, hold the end of it in your left hand, the bobbin in your right with its head to the left. Lay the thread round your left forefinger, first under, then over, to form a loop. Withdraw your finger. Insert the head of the bobbin in the loop and draw the thread tight. This loop is what is generally known as a half-hitch.

To wind a pair of bobbins with one thread, wind the first bobbin as directed, then tell off what you think a suitable length of thread for the second bobbin. Generally three or four yards will be enough ; with coarse thread less, with fine more goes under the bobbin-cover. Thread on to this length of thread the second bobbin-cover the opposite way round from the first one. Then wind the second bobbin, starting from the end of the thread and ending with the second half-hitch some six inches from the first. It is always neatest and best to wind bobbins pairwise in this manner, for shaped pieces especially.

Winding by machine need hardly be explained : once the bobbin is fixed, secure the thread by hand with a few turns towards you, then turn the wheel away from you.

The bobbins when wound are hung over the pins according to the pattern instructions. If they have not been wound double, knot them in groups for each pin. They will most likely hang unevenly ; this is very inconvenient in working and leads to constant tangles. Bring them all to one level by lengthening or shortening the thread, and always keep them level as you work. There should be about three inches of thread between the pin and the bobbin head.

To lengthen your available thread, hold the bobbin in your right hand so that it forms a right angle with the thread (the half-hitch must be just at the bobbin's head), then between your thumb and forefinger roll the bobbin from left to right, keeping the thread taut.

To shorten your thread, hold the bobbin as before. Take between the thumb and forefinger of your left hand the part of the thread that passes down the bobbin ; draw it outwards from the bobbin, holding all taut the while, and turn the bobbin from right to left between the thumb and forefinger of your right hand.

These manœuvres, extremely simple as they are, require a little practice. On first hanging, the bobbins are prone to unwind themselves. To prevent this, some put the loop of the half-hitch twice round the head of each, but that is hardly to be recommended as it interferes with the lengthening and shortening. A little patience is the better method, and the beginner soon ceases to have any trouble with altering the lengths.

Now you are ready to begin work.

CHAPTER VI

THE VARIETIES OF PILLOW LACE

But the Beaver went on making lace, and displayed
  No interest in the concern,
Though the Barrister tried to appeal to its pride,
  And vainly proceeded to cite
A number of cases in which making laces
  Had been proved an infringement of right.
                LEWIS CARROLL: "The Hunting of the Snark."

PILLOW LACE may be divided into four classes :
    1. TAPE LACE. The design is formed of a tape
curved so as to make a mazy fabric. "Russian lace"
is the modern representative of this class, which in
the seventeenth century flourished most in Flanders
and Genoa.

2. PLAITED LACE. The design is of lines made
with one, or more often two, pair of bobbins, and
these lines form the basis of the whole fabric. This
was common in the sixteenth and seventeenth centuries—indeed, most of the pillow-lace pattern-books
of the time contain little else. The style is now
seldom seen, but it can produce very good effects.

3. GROUNDED LACE. The design consists of solid
figures, standing out more or less plainly from a
lighter net background. To this class belongs much
of the high aristocracy of pillow lace—Chantilly,
Mechlin, Valenciennes, and silk blonds.

4. GUIPURE. The design is of solid figures connected, not by a net background, but by plaits and twists. This class includes some of the most charming laces and many varieties, a group of French laces (Cluny, Mirecourt, and Le Puy), Maltese, Bohemian, and Saxon, down to the Italian peasant laces represented by Rapallese.

There is another kind of guipure in higher repute, which blends with our first class of tape laces, since its solid figures are formed of modifications of tape. To this belong our Honiton and the Belgian laces, Brussels, Duchesse, and Bruges.

"Guipure" is a French word, which was first used to indicate a lace the figures of which were emphasized by an outline of "gimp," a coarser thread or fine cord. The term is nowadays, like most other terms in lace, very loosely applied ; but on the whole the above is now its recognized meaning, the opposite to guipure being "dentelle à réseau"=grounded lace, or more simply "dentelle." Both in England and Germany, native terms mark no such trenchant division, and as the distinction is actual and a useful guide in the intricacies of classification, we have kept the word "guipure" familiarized by drapers, and translate the opposite term.

These four classes often shade into one another in their varieties. Tape laces, for instance, can have their tapes connected in part by means of groundwork or by means of plaits. Grounded laces (such as the so-called "point de Milan" or the Valenciennes de Brabant) may have their figures formed by tapes which are afterwards joined by the addition of grounding. We have already seen how guipure shades off into tape lace; and plaits may be used in connexion with grounds, as is so frequently the case in the patterns of " Le Pompe."[1]

It falls outside the scope of this book to give details of the characteristics of all the different varieties of pillow lace. We can the more readily dismiss the subject, as it has been admirably treated in "Point and Pillow Lace" by Miss Mary Sharp, which gives photographs of characteristic specimens of all classes, with valuable observations. A good deal may be learnt too from A. Lefébure, though he has made some mistakes in classification, even confusing point with pillow. Far more trustworthy are the beautiful illustrations in Séguin and those of Mrs. Bury Palliser. Above all, the student of lace should go to museums, observe, compare, and not put too blind a trust in the labels on the cases.

The reason why we are not for the present concerned with this fascinating work of classifying, is that the aim of this book is to guide the lace-*maker*, not the connoisseur, and the worker still in need of such guidance has no concern with what most interests the student. For most of the famous kinds of pillow lace do not lend themselves to amateur handling. The number of bobbins needed is in many cases excessive; Mechlin of no great width requires five hundred, and such a number exacts a dexterity that only comes of constant practice.

[1] See above, p. 17, and the middle pattern of Fig. 1.

Valenciennes, Brussels, and Honiton make great demands on eyesight and patience. Chantilly, Mechlin,
Valenciennes, and Lille have all been made banal
by an infinity of very accurate machine-made copies,[1]
and even were this not the case their patterns as
a whole are not effective. The essentially English
laces are, except Honiton, unattractive models save
for their local interest.

In our choice of types and patterns we have aimed
at the greatest possible variety of such as would set
no great strain on eyesight or patience. And we have
tried to reduce to a minimum the number of laces
in which it is constantly necessary to cut out bobbins
and hang in fresh pairs, that process being not only
vexatious, but weakening to the fabric.

The beginner generally starts with Torchon lace ;
our experience goes to show that Russian lace is
more easily acquired. Once a simple form of "tape "
is mastered, and the way of curving and joining
it learnt, many laces can be made forthwith without
any further difficulty. We have therefore put the
Russian laces first. But in case any one prefers to
begin with the Torchon laces (chapter VIII), we have
commenced that chapter with the simplest possible
forms, given very full explanations, and carefully
graded the laces in order of difficulty.

[1] According to Séguin, "le plus fin connaisseur ne les distinguerait seulement
pas d'une imitation à une faible distance."

CHAPTER VII

RUSSIAN LACE

Wer noch nichts kan, noch g'lernet hat,
Dem ist es drumb kein Schand noch Schad ;
Aber wer nichts will lernen than,
Der soll den Spott zum Schaden han.

(Old Pattern-book).

THIS is the most usual name for a kind of lace, simple and often very beautiful. In Germany it [is sometimes called Idrian lace ; we have also seen the name "Genoese point" given to it, but that is a clear misnomer, for the essence of "point" is that it should be needlework. So for want of any better name we will call it Russian, though it certainly is not of Russian origin. It appears to originate in Genoa in the late sixteenth century, and took root in the early seventeenth century in Flanders, its head-quarters for many years. Russia seems to have learnt it much later from Flemish workers brought over by Peter the Great. But, despite its late introduction, Russia has now most claim to this lace, since not only are most Russian laces of this kind, but comparatively little is made elsewhere.

The special character of Russian lace is given it by its formation from one, sometimes two, or at most three narrow bands so curved and recurved as to

make a wide fabric. Those places where the bands
do not touch are filled by some form of grounding
made either with bobbins temporarily withdrawn
from the bands and returned again without cutting
of threads, or by a few additional bobbins hung in and
cut out again as the pattern requires. It is an easy
lace, because there are few stitches to be learnt and
few bobbins to worry the beginner. For it must be
admitted, half her difficulties come from the dreadful
way the bobbins have of knotting and twisting themselves into ugly patterns of their own. With few to
manage it is easier to keep discipline, so Russian lace
is good to begin upon. The narrow Torchons usually
chosen for that purpose are no easier and far less
tempting.

The pillows which can be used for Russian lace are
the Belgian mushroom-shape (Fig. 24), the flat cushion
(Fig. 37), and the large Honiton sphere (Fig. 27).
Those intended for ordinary yard-work are unsuitable,
as this lace presupposes working not in one direction,
but backwards and forwards, to right or left as the
curves of the pattern determine. And as the direction
changes the position of the pillow must change.

The commonest form of band used in Russian lace
is a combination of cloth-stitch and twistings. The
beginner had best first master the art of cloth-stitch.

CLOTH-STITCH. Fasten a piece of squared paper
(about 2 in. by 3 in.) upon your pillow. Set a row of
five pins, each two squares apart, across the head of
the paper. Hang a pair of bobbins on each pin.
See that the bobbins hang evenly—that is to say, that

the head of each bobbin is about three inches from the pin. Starting from the left, take pair 1 in your left hand, pair 2 in your right ; place the right bobbin of 1 over the left bobbin of 2 ; then the left of 2 over the left of 1 and the right of 2 over the right of 1 ; and finally the left of 1 over the right of 2. That is the whole stitch, and it should look like Fig. 33.

Hang 2 over a long pin set some four inches from the pins on the left-hand side. Repeat the process described with 3, 3 taking the place of 2. Hang 3 over the long pin. Proceed with 4, then with 5. This done, set a pin one square below the first pin on the right, and let 1 fall to the right of it and 5 to the left. Now return backwards in precisely the same way, using 1 all the time as the weft of your fabric, or, as the lace-makers call it, the "workers." The other pairs which these must cross are called the "passives." Set your pins in straight vertical lines, each pin one square lower than the last on the opposite side. Hang each pair of bobbins out of your way over the large pins at the side when you have finished with it. Never twist your threads, and the cloth will look just like darning or plain weaving. Work to and fro many times until you are so familiar with the stitch as to make it mechanically.

MAKING THE TAPE. The tape which forms the pattern of Russian lace can be made in several ways :

1. It may be a simple band of cloth-stitch (Fig. 36, a), or a double band of cloth-stitch with two pairs of workers which constantly meet to part again in the middle of the tape.

2. The most frequent form (Fig. 36, b) is slightly more complex, involving the operation of twisting.

TWISTING is placing the right thread of a pair over the left of its own pair. Remember it is always the *right* that goes over.

Hang three pairs at A, two at B, and one at C. Start with the left-hand pair at B.[1] Twist it, pass it in cloth-stitch through the three pairs hanging from A. (Always hang each pair, as you finish with it, out of your way over a long pin, so that you have always only two pairs in hand at once, and so avoid confusion.)

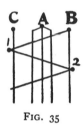

FIG. 35

Twist again; twist also the pair hanging from C. Make a cloth-stitch with these two pairs. Set pin No. 1 between them. Cloth-stitch again to close the pin. Twist the workers, c.s.[2] again through the three passive pairs; twist again, twist the pair hanging from B, c.s., set pin No. 2, close the pin with c.s., and so on.

Almost all Russian laces are made with this tape, which is also the basis of Bruges and Honiton. It adapts itself best to the crochet-hook, which plays such an important part in these laces.

[1] The right-hand pair at B and the pair at C are called the "outer pairs."
[2] Cloth-stitch.

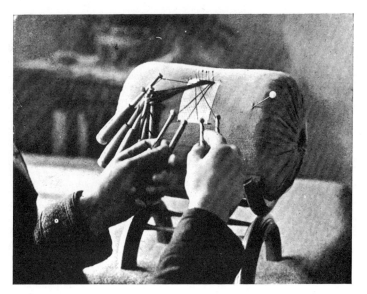

FIG. 33. MAKING CLOTH-STITCH. (GERMAN PILLOW AND STAND)

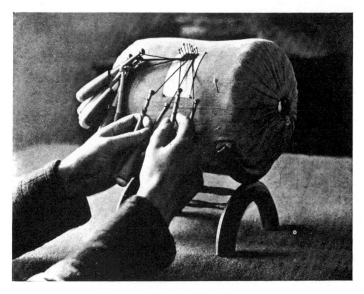

FIG. 34. MAKING HALF-STITCH

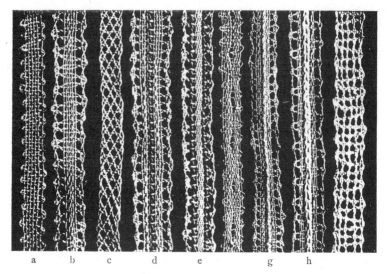

a   b   c   d   e   g   h

FIG. 36. VARIOUS FORMS OF TAPE

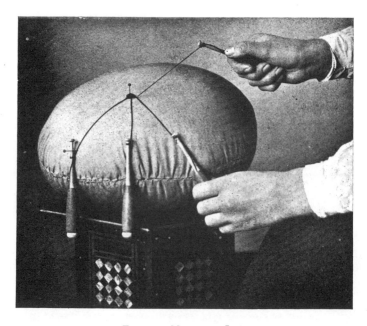

FIG. 37. MAKING A LEAF

3. Plain half-stitch[1] (Fig. 36, c) is sometimes used here and there to vary the tape, but rarely, and seldom with good effect. We will therefore leave it out of consideration for the present.

4. The other varieties of tape are all variants of No. 2. A raised appearance (Fig. 36, d, e) may be produced by introducing one or two coarse threads among the passives. If one is used it will lie in the middle of the passives; if two, they can be either together in the middle or (in a straight tape) one at each edge.

5. In the same way coloured thread can be introduced. This serves to accentuate the design where the lace is close woven and intricate, also to make the lace match in colour the embroidery or the dress which it trims.

6. Twisting the workers in different ways varies the tape. Twisting them twice or even, with very fine thread, three times between the passives and the outer pairs makes the lace firmer and more wiry. In such cases the outer pairs should be twisted correspondingly. Twisting the workers between the two centre pairs of passives here and there forms little holes which lighten the tape (Fig. 36, f).

7. All the passives may be twisted at regular intervals. Or if a coarse pair be employed in the middle this may be twisted each time above the workers and these latter simply passed between the two coarse threads. The result is like a twisted cord running down the middle of the tape (Fig. 36, g).

---

[1] See below, p. 117.

8. This proceeding may be doubled to obtain the appearance of a raised plait (Fig. 36, h). There must be two pairs with coarse thread; the right-hand pair is invariably twisted toward the left and the left-hand pair toward the right. German workers call this "Kettelschlag," chain-stitch.

9. Both workers and passives may be twisted before every stitch (Fig. 36, i). This is an effective variation, giving lightness to the tape.

SHAPING THE TAPE. Having learned how to make the tape, we must now see about forming patterns with it. To do this we must be able to go round curves and angles. Herein lies half the superiority of Russian over the so-called Renaissance lace, that kind of point that is made from braids. The one is bound to be more or less clumsy and thick where it is gathered to form curves or folded for angles; the other, infinitely more graceful and flowing in effect, adapts itself without effort to these shapings.

Curves, right angles, and obtuse angles. It is evident that round a curve one edge of the tape grows disproportionately long while the other shortens. The long edge needs just as many crossings from the workers to support it as before, but in the short there is not room for so many. It follows then that the workers must, towards the middle of the curve, only partially cross the passives and avoid the inner edge. To do this, proceed till the workers cross the last pair of passives, then take these as workers, leaving the old workers in their place, and work back again to the outer edge of the curve, leaving the twisted pair on the inner edge untouched.

To form a sharp-pointed angle, work as usual up to point A; there leave the outer pair out of your way, it will not be needed for some time. Work on to point B, there exchange the workers for the last pair of passives and hang the workers out of the way. From B to C continue dropping pairs in this way till you have only one pair of passives left. Then complete the re-

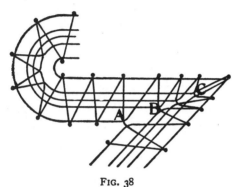

FIG. 38

maining half of the angle, taking up each neglected pair in turn as workers, till just before A, where the workers must again be twisted before exchanging with the pair left hanging at A. After this point all is plain sailing.

These two methods will adjust the tape to any form.

FORMING THE FABRIC. The tapes, made and shaped as we have seen, can be joined together in a variety of ways :

1. Sometimes a lace is made with two tapes, running, for a time at least, parallel to each other. The joining is effected by two passes of cloth-stitch (one

before the pin, one after) between the two pairs of workers.

2. But more often the tape, doubling on its own track, must be joined to one of its own parts. This is done with the help of a fine steel crochet-hook. Take away the pin from the hole in the finished edge, to which you wish to join your workers. Pass the crochet-hook downwards through the hole, and with it pull up one thread of the working pair till it forms a wide loop ; pass the other working bobbin tail foremost through this loop and draw both threads tight. The join will be perfectly firm. This, *lucus a non lucendo*, is called a sewing (in French, *crochetage*).

3. You may have to hang in fresh bobbins to fill up an open space with other kinds of work. To do this wind your pairs in one (see p. 80), and hang them over a pin near the place where they are to be inserted, a pin which can be almost instantly removed. Having brought your workers to the point from which the bobbins are to start, make one cloth-stitch across each new pair, and then let them hang out of the way, continuing with your workers till the piece of tape in question is firmly woven. Remove the pin from which the new pairs hang, draw them into position, and proceed with them.

Three kinds of filling are in constant use. One, the various grounds,[1] we do not recommend to beginners, as they involve hanging in and cutting out many pairs of bobbins, a troublesome and weakening process. More effective are leaves and plaits.

[1] See below, Torchon, p. 123 ; Rose, p. 142.

Plaits are very easy and quickly made; they take two pair. Start with a cloth-stitch,[1] twist both pairs, and then place the right thread of the left pair over the left thread of the right pair; alternately twist and repeat this operation until your plait is long enough. The plait may be ornamented and held in position in the making by *picots*, little loops formed by drawing the outer thread on the side where the picot is to lie, first below, then round and over the pin indicated for that purpose in the pattern.

Leaves, on the other hand, require some dexterity and practice, but they are such an immense improvement in all kinds of lace that no lace-maker can afford to neglect them. It is only the manipulation that is difficult; in theory nothing can be more simple. Two pair are required; take the left-hand bobbin of all and weave it to and fro, passing it alternately over and under each of the other three threads until the leaf is long enough. The difficulty consists in keeping the three warp threads at the right tension. This is best done by letting the centre one hang straight down, and hanging the two side ones over pins that keep them pretty much equidistant from the centre bobbin, the outer threads forming a right angle at the pin you start from. Keep the warp bobbins, especially the middle one, on shorter thread than usual, the weaver on a longer. Never let the two outer warps slip out of position, or the outline of the leaf will be broken. Form the shape of your leaf to taste, curving it out by stretching the

[1] See p. 88 f.

outer warps and in again by tightening the weaver. It may be a leaf proper, either slim or broad, or else a square bar. The bar starts square, and is woven evenly all through its length ; the leaf starts from a point, widens in the middle, and decreases to a point at the bottom. It is better not to tighten it quite to its proper shape at the lower end, as the pulling of the threads to form whatever stitch ends the leaf will do this quite sufficiently. These leaves are used separately, or in groups forming the petals of a flower.

A fourth way of filling in the space between two tapes is suddenly to change the tape itself into some open grounding requiring the same number of bobbins. This is often done in broad Russian laces with effect and ingenuity. We mention the method here more for the sake of completeness and as a suggestion to the practised worker for new designs than as of use to the beginner.

Having learned all the movements which go to making Russian lace,[1] we must now put them in practice, beginning with a very simple lace of a single tape.

No. 1.—*Trimming for a Dress*

This pattern, which is neither lace nor insertion, but something of both, comes from Russia. It is suited for trimming linen dresses and blouses, and may be worked with coloured thread for the centre pair of

---

[1] Cloth-stitch and the common form of tape should be practised till quite familiar before proceeding.

passives, as illustrated, or without. That is a matter
of taste ; personally we prefer the white version,
but the colour of the dress itself introduced into the
trimming might have a very good effect.

The pattern, which is quickly worked, lends itself
equally well to thread or silk. It may be worked
with Taylor's Mecklenburg thread No. 4. If the
introduction of a colour is desired, use a medium size

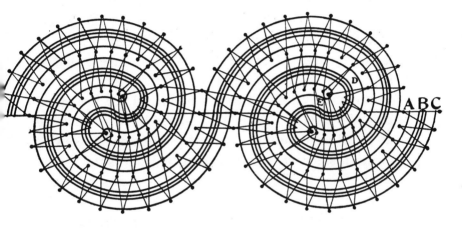

of lustrine, having first tested the fastness of the dye
by steeping a sample in hot soda and water.

Trace the above pattern twice on separate pieces
of tracing-cloth;[1] these will be used alternately, care
being taken that the lines join exactly. By the time
you have worked to the end of the first "repeat,"
you can begin taking pins out from the beginning to
use again ; so before you have worked to the end
of the second pattern, the first is ready to be used
again below the second. Each dot of the diagram

[1] See p. 73.

represents a pin, each line a pair of threads. It will not be necessary to indicate the dots in your tracing, nor any of the lines that represent the passives.

Six pairs of bobbins are needed. Hang one at A, three at B, two at C. The tape is the common one, No. 2, described on p. 90, which you have already practised ; one pair of C are the workers. There are several inches of plain tape before any complications occur. Follow it from A B C round to D, and in working it twist the outer pair once where the pin-holes are close together, but twice where they are further apart. After D the curve in the lace is sharper, and must be worked as described on p. 92 ; the workers are three times interchanged for the inmost pair of passives. After that comes the first "sewing" at E. As the tape winds round, there will be sewings on both sides wherever the diagram shows the workers of two parts of the tape coming to the same point. Note that wherever the outer edge of a curve lies along the inner edge of its neighbour, the latter has more holes, so that there are not sewings into all of these.

No. 2.—Insertion for a Blouse

This pattern is adapted from the design of a lace made by Russian peasants, but it has been simplified for the beginner, who will find it quite easy. Its only advance in difficulty on the preceding pattern is that here the worker learns to manage a greater number of bobbins, fourteen pair, for there are three tapes instead of one. In the model, Taylor's Mecklenburg thread No. 10 was used. This insertion would harmonize well with lace No. 3 if each were worked in the same thread, the lace made finer, or the insertion coarser; they could then trim the same costume. If a corner-piece is desired, it can be made as suggested on page 75.

Hang six pair at A, four at B, four at C. The centre tape is the same type as in the pattern already given, with outer twisted pairs; the two outside tapes are of simple cloth-stitch. The three passives of the centre tape are indicated by a single line, in order

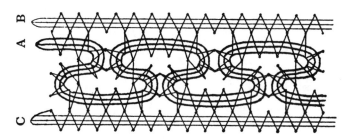

not to blur the small diagram. Follow carefully the direction lines; see to it that your tapes shape well round the curves; work with slack tension (i.e. do not tug the workers tight at the pins, nor the passives as the workers cross them), and the insertion cannot be a failure.

No. 3.—Lace for a Tea-cloth

This pattern, which comes to us from Berlin, might be turned to a variety of uses. It would serve equally well as trimming to tea, sideboard, or tray cloth, to a blouse or a toilet-cover. Like No. 2, with which it might be used, it lends itself to forming a corner,[1] and a little ingenuity would soon adapt it to a round d'oyley edging to match the suggested cloths.

It requires six pair of bobbins, and the actual model was worked with Taylor's Mecklenburg lace thread No. 2 ; but it might also be made with much finer thread.

Hang on one pair at A, three at B, two at C. Make a cloth-stitch with the two pairs of C. With the left-hand of these two pairs as workers, proceed

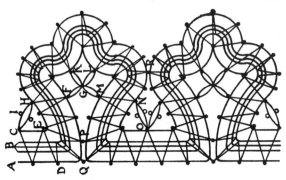

to work the tape as described on page 90, till you come to the point D. Now make the curve by the method described (p. 92), the workers being twice exchanged for the last passives. This brings you to the point E, where the workers must be joined by a sewing (see p. 94) to the loop already made here. Continue the tape to F. When you have made the cloth-stitch with the workers and the outside pair at F, twist the workers several times, pass them round a pin at G, twist again several times, and bring them back to make another cloth-stitch with the outer pair

[1] See p. 75.

Nos. 1, 2, AND 3.   RUSSIAN LACES

No. 4. RUSSIAN INSERTION
No. 5. RUSSIAN LACE

at F. Continue through the tape to H. After setting the pin at H, make a plait (p. 95) with the workers and the outer pair. The plait must be long enough to reach to C, and at I a picot must be made (see p. 95). Fasten the plait by a sewing into the loop already made at C; in the case of a plait, *both* threads of one pair must be drawn through with the crochet-hook, and the second pair passed through the loop thus made. Make a second plait, with picot, back to H, and fasten it by a sewing. Continue the tape, following the lines of the diagram. At K and L, as at F, the workers must be twisted and carried out to G and back. At N a plait must be carried to O and back. At M twist the workers, carry them to G, and crochet them through the three loops from F, K, and L. At P and Q the second curve will be fastened to the first by sewing. At O the workers of the tape are fastened to the plait, and at R the second vandyke is secured to the first.

No. 4.—Greek Key Insertion

This pattern, though it requires more pairs of bobbins (twenty-one) than most Russian laces, is such plain sailing in all other respects that an inexperienced worker can well venture on it. It is most effective for use in house-linen, on sheets, down the centre of a sideboard-cloth, etc., or for window-blinds. It should be worked in coarse thread—for instance, Harris's 20 2-cord—when it will be found to be everlasting wear.

Hang one pair of bobbins at A, four at B, one at

C, two at D, one at E, four at F, one at G, one at H, four at I, two at K; i.e. seven pair for each

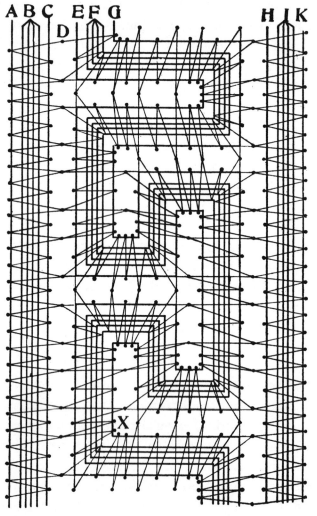

tape, two outer pairs, four pair of passives, and one of workers to each.

The "repeat" of the pattern is from A to X.

No. 5.—*Medium Lace*

This pattern requires fourteen pair of bobbins, and can be worked with Mecklenburg thread No. 4. Being very firm and lasting, it is suited for house-linen, teacloths, sheets, etc., and is quite handsome enough to trim a dress.

In both tapes there are *four* inner pairs of passives; only two are shown in the diagram. Hang two pair at A, four at B, one at C, two at D, four at E, one at F. Different as is the pattern from No. 3, there is so much analogy in the working that any one who has mastered the former will find no difficulty here.

At G the outer pair of the inner curve is early taken in as a passive to give a lighter, more open effect. At the centre H do not attempt to loop your plaits into one another until the last plait reaches that point and loops in all the other three at once.

No. 6.—*End of a Tie*

A Russian model this, which will finish the end of a tie, or serve as *motif* for insertion. The original was worked in Barbour's thread No. 70 2-cord; it would also bear working coarser, e.g. with Taylor's No. 4.

Seven pairs are required. Hang two at A, four at B, one at C, all threaded pairwise, so that the final join in the lace may be invisible. The four inner passives are indicated in the diagram by two lines only. Work round to the right; the direction lines of the diagram explain sufficiently the way of working until point D is reached. Here with the workers and the outer pair make a leaf (see p. 95) long enough to reach to the centre of the flower. Set a pin in that centre, bring your bobbins round to the right, and let one pair fall to each side of the pin. Make a cloth-stitch with them below the pin to fix all firm, and proceed to make another leaf the same size. When this is finished set a pin at E, let one pair fall to each side of the pin, close with a cloth-stitch and proceed as usual. After point F take in the outer pairs to the body of the tape, making a plain cloth-stitch tape until K, the corresponding point on the opposite side, where the

ordinary tape begins again. At G, make with the
workers and the outer pairs a leaf long enough to
touch the centre of the flower. Make a second leaf

and bring it back to H. Continue the tape as at E.
At I, another pair of leaves as at G. At K, make a
plait of the workers and the last passives, fasten it to

L by sewing, continue the plait to M, a pin at M
between the two pairs, and so alternately by fresh pins
and sewings back to F.   Then return to K, making
sewings all the way as far as N, after that alternate
sewings and fresh pins.   From K resume the ordinary
tape.   At O make a leaf as at D, G, I, fasten it by a
sewing (with the loop made of one pair, the tie thread
of the other) through all the three pairs of leaves
already there, and another leaf back to P.   There
are no further difficulties.   Having reached A B C,
cut all the threads four inches from the pins, pass one
thread of each pair through the loop of the corresponding pair at the start, and finish by a reef-knot on
the wrong side of the lace.

No. 7.—D'oyley

This pattern with slight alterations gives four
d'oyleys—two round, two square.   First let us take
the square one (pattern 7a on Sheet 1).

Harris's 20 2-cord thread.   Hang four pair at B, two
at A, two at C.   Later on, four additional pairs will
be needed, twelve in all; or if you wish the outer
plait shown in the illustration, two more must be hung
at A, fourteen then in all.

Start from A; at C form a plait with the workers
and outer pair, take it round a pin at D and back to
C, not forgetting the picots, which greatly improve it.
Both at E and F take another plait round the pin at
D, and back again into the tape.   At G a similar
plait loops by a sewing into pinhole F, and at H
another is fastened by a sewing through all three

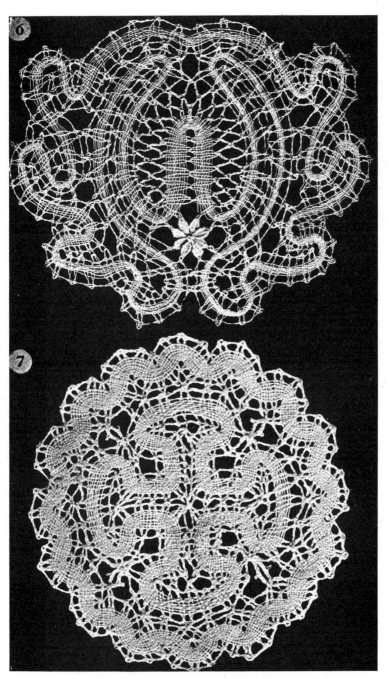

No. 6. RUSSIAN TIE-END
No. 7. RUSSIAN ROUND D'OYLEY

No. 7a. RUSSIAN SQUARE D'OYLEY (reduced)

loops at D. At I is the last plait of the corner which
fastens into C.

At J hang on four more pair, two of which form
the circle of plaiting, the other two the ring of leaves.
The first leaf goes to K and the second returns to L,
where it is joined to the tape after the plait of the
circle has been passed between its two pair. Then
a third leaf goes to M, and so on all round the circle.

At N take out a loop of plaiting to O, at P one to
Q, and at R another to S. Having reached T, the
tape parts from the centre work ; the leaf pairs proceed to U, where they are joined by another leaf
coming from J formed of the two pairs of the plait,
which are fastened to J by a sewing.

At U take out a plait to V and back to W, joining
it across the second circle of plait starting at U by
sewings to W and the succeeding points on the circle.
Having worked round to K, take one plait out to X
and the other to U, fasten it there by a sewing and
bring it to join the other at X.

From X take a plait round the innermost circle,
fastening it by sewings to every alternate point, beginning with V. The other points will be secured as
before by sewings from the leaves, but this innermost
star of leaves is made double ; the first leaf goes from
X to the centre of the star, the second returns to Y,
the third goes back from Y to the centre and out
again to Z, whence it returns again to the centre, and
so on. Each pair of leaves is fastened to the preceding pair by a sewing. At X knot off all four pairs
of bobbins.

PATTERN No. 7

Continue your tape. At 2 take out a loop of plait to 1 and another to S. The rest is perfectly plain sailing. Finish at A B C as in No. 6.

The round d'oyley is shown in the diagram on page 108. The waved border is worked just as in the square one. For the centre in the form of a cross, hang one pair at A, three at B (the centre one may, if desired, be wound with coloured thread), two at C; the lines sufficiently indicate the mode of working.

Two varieties may be made by interchanging the centres of the two patterns, which offers no difficulty.

No. 8.—Wide Lace for a Dress

This model comes from the Erzgebirge. The disadvantage of the many joins is compensated by its handsome and unusual design, and by the fact that the outer rings can be formed separately and the lower part of the border made without them. This and its fine texture adapt it for a dress trimming, for we have at once two widths of lace, a medallion, and an insertion formed of medallions, all to match.

Mecklenburg thread No. 10 is used. For the footing, six pair are needed in two equal bands of c.s., whose workers interlace after being twice twisted. For the rest, eight pair all hung at A, where you start with c.s. The characteristic point of this lace is that at the inner point of each curve the outer pair is twisted and then taken into the passives. On starting at A, the first part is a plain c.s. tape; and on the inside of the little circle the workers are each time ex-

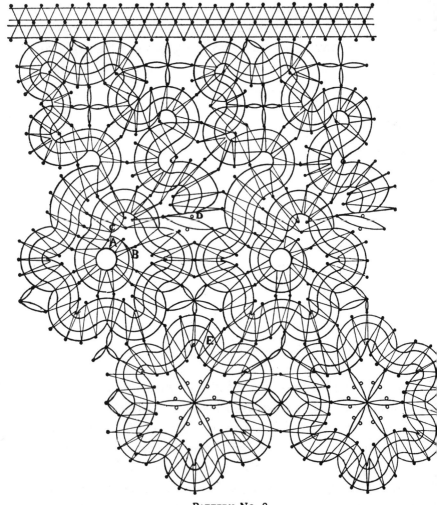

PATTERN No. 8

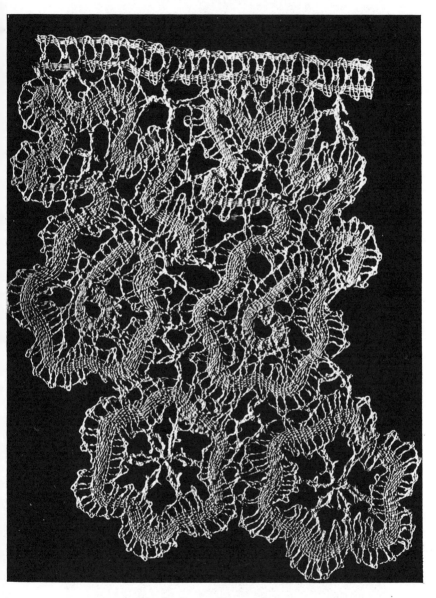

No. 8. Broad Russian Lace

No. 9. RUSSIAN TRIANGLE (reduced)

changed for the innermost pair of passives. After B, one of the passives is taken outside the tape (i.e. the workers are twisted between it and the others), and after C, a pair on the other side is taken out, so that from this on (except, as we have said, at the inside of curves) the tape is the ordinary form. On coming round to A again, connect the workers by a sewing with the loops of thread at A. Continue this tape, making the connecting loops of plait as in No. 7 where the diagram shows, to D; here the threads must be cut and fastened as neatly as possible. Hang them on for the lower ring at E; on working round again to E they have to be cut again.

No. 9.—*Triangle* (*see Sheet* 1)

Complicated as this triangle looks, it is all worked with seven pair of bobbins. Wind them in pairs with Mecklenburg thread No. 4, and hang one pair at A, four at B, two at C; and, taking one pair of C as workers, begin the tape in the usual way. The connecting plaits may be worked in the same way as in the square d'oyley (No. 7), or here is an alternative way which some workers may prefer: On reaching 1, make a plait with the workers and the outer pair of passives to 2, thence back and round pin 1 again, and continue, taking the pins in the following order: 3, 4, back to 3, 5, 6, back to 5, back to 3, 7, 8, back to 7, back to 3, and here connect with the other three loops of plait at this point by a sewing, back to 1, connect by a sewing with the original plait at 1, and then continue the tape as before. At 7, connect by sewing with the two loops there. At 9, make a plait to 10 and back. At 10, 8, 5, connect with the loops. On reaching 11, plait the workers and passives, and take the plait round pins in the following order : 12, back to 11, 13, 14, back to 13, 15, 16, back to 15, back to 13, 17, 18, 19, 20, back to 19, 21, back to 19, 22, back to 19 and connect with the other three, 18, 17, 13, and connect with the other three, back to 11, and continue the tape, connecting with the loops at 17 and 22. From 23, take a plait as before to 24, 25, 26, 27, back to 26, 28, 29, back to 28, 26, 30, 31, back to 30, 26, here connect with the other three loops, 25, 24, 23, and continue the tape, connecting with the loops at 25 and 31. At 32 take a plait to 33 and back.

Continue the tape, connecting with the loops at 33, 30, 28, till you come to 34, and from here work the centre of the flower with the workers and outer passives. Make leaves to 35, 36, 37, 38, 39, 40, 41, 42, a plait to 43 and back to 42, a plait to 44 and back to 42, connecting with the previous loop. Then leaves to 45, 46, 47, 48, 49, 50, 51. From 51 a plait to 52 on the centre ring, to 35 and connect with the leaves, and so on to and fro from the points on the centre ring to 37, 39, 41, 45, 47, 49, till you reach 53. Then plait the centre ring, connecting with the loops of plait, till you come back to 53 ; connect here, make a plait to 51 and connect, then a leaf to 34 and connect. Now continue the tape, connecting with the loops at 29, 36, 27, 24, 38, 21, 20, 40, 43, till you come to 54. From 54 a plait to 55 and back, then continue the tape, connecting with the loops at 20, 18, 15, 55, and on to 56. Hence take a plait as before to 57, back to 56, 58, 59, back to 58, 60, back to 58, 61, 62, back to 61, 58, here connect with the other three, 56, and continue the tape, connecting with the loops at 61.

The second half of the triangle is worked much like the first. From 65 begin a system of plaits in the following order : 66, 65, 67, 68, 67, 69, 70, 69, 67, 71, 72, 73, 74, 73, 75, 73, 76, 73 (here connect with the other loops), 72, 71, 67 (here connect with the other loops), 65 (connect), and continue the tape, connecting with the loops. A plait goes from 77 to 78 and back. The working of the system of plaits starting from 79, and the remaining ones of the pattern, is similar, and scarcely needs further explanation. Be sure you make all the connections, not leaving any loops of plait uncaught, and remember always the picots on the plaits. On working the tape to A B C, where you started from, cut off the bobbins and finish off in the usual way.

No. 10.—*Handkerchief* (*see Sheet* 1)

Thread, Barbour's 2-cord 80. Hang six pair at A and begin working a c.s. tape. This tape has the peculiarity that the pairs of passives at the right edge and the left are both twisted once ; further, that on the edge touching the linen square of the handkerchief the workers are exchanged for the last pair of passives, which they meet in a simple whole stitch.[1] If, however, this system is found confusing, both edges of the tape may quite well be worked alike.

Continue your tape to B, whence you take out a leaf to C, the centre of the flower, and back into the tape at D. This flower is made in the same way as that at point D in No. 6, save that having more petals, these cannot be all joined by one sewing, but each pair of petals must be attached to the pair last made by a fresh sewing.

At E, proceed with the workers and the last pair of passives to make the net filling. This is done by taking the passives straight along the line E F, and alternately fastening the workers by a sewing to the tape and by two whole stitches to the passives, one before the pin, one after. Each pair is twisted once between each operation. Having in this way reached F, take both pairs together in a loose plait to G, and return in much the same way by alternate sewings and fresh pins to H, where you resume your tape. This process is repeated at I, the pairs returning to K, at L, the pairs returning to M, and finally at N, the pairs returning to O.

The rest of the work is simple; indeed, the only difficulty of this apparently elaborate piece of work is the keeping of a loose enough tension.

---

[1] See below, p. 120.

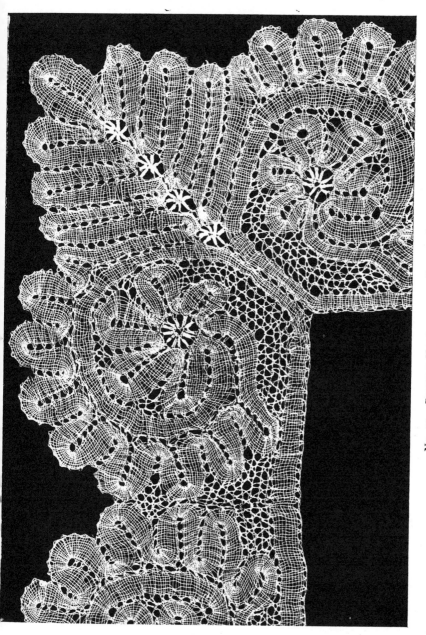

No. 10. Russian Handkerchief Border (reduced)

CHAPTER VIII

TORCHON

Quand l'art de faire la dentelle seroit perdu, ce que je viens de dire suffiroit seul pour qu'il fut très-facile de le retrouver.

DIDEROT-D'ALEMBERT'S "Encyclopædia."

RUSSIAN lace has salient characteristics and well-defined limitations; not so Torchon, which shades off into Maltese, into Cluny, and other laces of a higher grade than its own. Torchon is the cheapest of all pillow lace; its very name a reproach, meaning a clout or dish-cloth. An older name for it was Gueuse, beggar-woman's lace. Without sharing so uncomplimentary an opinion of Torchon, we must own that for an amateur of any ambition this lace must be chiefly a training, a transition to more complex patterns. It can be bought so cheaply everywhere. However, it is easy and amusing to make, and there is no more durable or prettier trimming for underclothes, so that the worker has plenty of use for any quantity she produces. Besides, it cannot be bought with square corners for handkerchiefs or tray-cloths, and these are a great improvement both to edgings and insertions. It is well worth while to make them, in order to avoid the clumsiness of gathered corners.

The design of Russian lace itself forms the fabric

of the lace without essential aid from any background. Torchon, on the other hand, is an example of the *dentelle à réseau*, "grounded lace"; not the most characteristic example, since the pattern may be said to consist more in a combination of grounds than in a design standing out from a background. The other grounded laces are not for the most part suited to the amateur, least of all the beginner. Of extremely fine thread, they require an infinity of bobbins, an infinity of time and patience, to say nothing of dexterity and eyesight. Valenciennes is the only kind usually attempted by amateurs; it is troublesome to make, and when done, only close inspection can distinguish it from machine-made lace. Torchon, on the contrary, is less successfully imitated in the cheap laces on the market. The machines generally in use can imitate cloth-stitch, but not half-stitch, which, infrequent in Valenciennes, plays so great a part in Torchon.

While Torchon cannot be separated from certain other pillow laces by a hard and fast line, it yet has certain features of its own. The patterns are invariably geometrical, and generally marked by most of their lines running "on the cross" of the lace. Lozenges play a great part in the designs; so do "spiders" and "fans." Except for these last and for other varieties of scallop all used on the outer edge, true Torchons have practically no curved lines. Nor is there, with very little exception, any raised work in them, though "bars" are used on the flat. Both laces and insertions are generally narrow. From this it may be easily seen that the chief beauty of

Torchon must consist in fineness of thread and even-
ness of working. The ease and quickness with which
it can be made is due partly to the narrowness of the
lace, partly to its open texture. The worker never
need turn her pillow, she works straight ahead;
therefore the common cylindrical pillow is best for
Torchons.

Most of the Torchon patterns given here were
brought from Malta, which is quite a centre of the
industry. A great deal is also made in Saxony and
Switzerland, besides different parts of Russia, France,
and Spain. Of course, wherever pillow lace is made
Torchon patterns are sometimes used, especially
by children and beginners; but in England less
than elsewhere, even the narrowest patterns in use
in Buckinghamshire being more of the nature of
Maltese.

The following examples have been carefully graded,
so that not more than one new feature is introduced
in each, and the worker thus contends with only one
difficulty at a time.

No. 11.—Narrow Lace

This is a pretty lace for trimming underclothing
when worked in fine thread. Taylor's Mecklenburg
lace thread No. 10 was used for the model. Eleven
pairs of bobbins are required. The lace is principally
composed of "*half-stitch,*" and this the learner must
practise before proceeding to make the lace. Fasten
a piece of squared paper, about two inches wide and
three long, to the cushion. Set five pins in it, two

squares apart, in a horizontal line; hang a pair of
bobbins on each, taking care that their heads are
hanging on a level. Starting from the left, take a
pair of bobbins in each hand. Twist each pair from
right to left, so that the right-hand thread passes
over the left. Then exchange what is now the right-
hand bobbin of the left pair for the left-hand bobbin
of the right pair in such a way that the former
passes over the latter. This is a "half-stitch"
(Fig. 34). Now lay aside the pair in your left

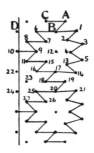

hand, hanging them over a long pin set some
inches from the pattern, so as to be out of your
way. Transfer the pair in your right hand to your
left, take up the third pair in your right, and twist
and pass over the bobbins as before to make another
half-stitch. Hang up the left-hand pair, and continue
as before, taking up the fourth pair, then the fifth.
After making the half-stitch with the last two pairs,
set a pin between them one square below the fifth pin.
Now return backwards in exactly the same way,
taking the pairs as they come, and hanging up each
pair as it is done with on a long pin some inches to

the right of the pattern. On making the half-stitch with the last two pairs on the left, set a pin between them two squares below the first pin, and return towards the right. Continue working to and fro, and setting the pins alternately on the right and left two squares below the previous one, till you are quite familiar with the stitch. You will see by looking at the fabric if you have made mistakes : if properly worked, one thread will pass backwards and forwards from pin to pin, while the others run in straight diagonal lines.

It does not often occur in a lace that the half-stitch fabric is worked continuously with the same set of pairs : it usually happens either that a pair is left aside after each pin is set, so as to reduce the number of pairs, or else a pair coming from another part of the lace is taken up before each pin so as to increase the number, or else pairs may be left off at one side while new pairs are taken in at the other. This will be seen in the first lace, which you can now proceed to work. Note that a pin is never left with the bobbins simply hanging on each side of it ; a stitch must be made below it with the pairs on each side. This is called closing the pin.

Trace the diagram twice over on tracing-linen. When you have worked to the end of one tracing, you can put the other on the pillow below it, taking care that the pattern joins properly on the two, and proceed to work over the second. By the time you have worked the second the pins can be taken out of the first, and it in its turn placed below the second.

Hang three pairs at A, two at B, three at C, three
at D—eleven in all. With one pair of B make half-
stitch with each of the three pairs of A in turn, twisting the last pair twice instead of once (this is to make
the outer edge firmer); set a pin at 1. Return
through the same three pairs to 2, set a pin, make
a half-stitch below the pin, and leave off the left-hand
pair. With the other three pairs continue the h.s.[1]
braid to 3, 4, 5, remembering on coming each time to
the edge to twist the outside pair twice.

Take the remaining pair of B, make h.s. with the
three pairs of C in turn, set a pin at 6; return to 7,
set a pin, h.s. below the pin, and leave off the right
pair. Return through the remaining pairs and take
up one pair of D; set a pin at 8; return to 9. From
9 return, making h.s. with these four pairs, then make
the *margin* thus : with the left-hand pair of the last
h.s. and the right-hand pair of D make a h.s. twice
over;[2] set a pin at 10, but do not as yet make a stitch
below it. Take the pair on the left of the pin and
the remaining pair of D, twist the latter twice, then
make a h.s. with them twice over. Leave the left-
hand pair. With the right-hand pair and the pair left
at 10 make a h.s. twice over below the pin ; leave the
left pair.

Begin again at point 9. Work h.s. with the four
pairs to 11.

Take up the pair left at 7 and the pair left at 2 ;
twist each twice, make h.s., set a pin at 12, another
h.s. below it, twist each pair twice.

---

[1] Half-stitch.   [2] This is called a whole-stitch.

Begin again at 5 and make h.s. with the three pairs left there, also with the right pair from 12 twisted twice; set a pin at 13. Return to 14, then back again through the four pairs, hanging up each pair as it is done with, and leaving the last one hanging by itself.

Begin again at 11, work to 15, taking up here the left pair from 12, twisted twice. Thence to 16, here leaving off a pair; thence to 17, taking in here the pair left hanging by itself on coming from 14; set a pin. Back to 18, then through all the seven pairs to 19. From 19 make h.s. with the first five pairs to 20, set a pin, h.s. below the pin, and hang up the left pair; with the right-hand pair return through the three pairs to 21, thence repeat as from point 1.

Take the pair left at 11, with it and the two marginal pairs make the edge at 22 as described at 10. Then take the right-hand of these three pairs, twist it twice; take also the pair left at 16, twisted twice, make h.s. with these two and set a pin at 23, make h.s. below the pin. With the left-hand pair and the two marginal pairs make the margin at 24 as before.

Take up the pair hung up at 20 and make h.s. with the pairs hanging on the left of 20, and take in also the right pair of 23 twisted twice: pin 25. Work back to 26, and here leave off a pair (as at 7), then back to 27, and here take in the right pair of 24 twisted twice. From 27 continue exactly as from 8.

No. 12.—Narrow Insertion

This insertion in its final form introduces Torchon-ground, cloth-stitch, and spider—all new to those who begin work with this chapter in preference to the Russian laces. In order that our readers may not have to learn all these at once, we give two simplified forms before coming to the final one. The first is composed of Torchon-ground along with the half-stitch

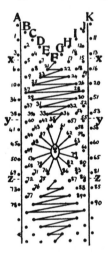

already practised; the second of cloth-stitch and Torchon-stitch; the third introduces the spider. The plate shows all three forms. Each of the two simpler forms can quite well be used as it is, so that the beginner need not grudge making a considerable length of it. It is not necessary to trace different patterns. The "repeat" for the first two forms is from x to y; for the third from x to z; but the tracing made for the first two can easily be adapted for the

third by marking a pinhole in the centre of each
alternate lozenge, and neglecting the zigzag lines in
that one. All three forms require fourteen pairs and
Mecklenburg thread No. 10.

First form.—Torchon-ground.—Set five pins in a
piece of squared paper two squares apart (see diagram),
and hang two pairs of bobbins on each. Take one
pair of 1 and one of 2, and make a half-stitch, only
twisting each pair *twice* instead of once; set pin 6
and make a half-stitch below it. Take the other pair
of 2 and one of 3; make the Torchon-stitch again
(i.e. a half-stitch with the pairs twisted twice); set

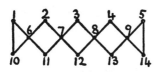

FIG. 39

pin 7 and make a half-stitch below. Do the same
with pairs from 3 and 4, setting pin 8, and with pairs
from 4 and 5, setting pin 9. Now take the remaining
pair of 1 and the left-hand pair of 6, make the Torchon-
stitch as before, and set pin 10; then the right
pair of 6 and the left of 7, and set pin 11, and so
on. Work several rows in this way till you are
familiar with the stitch. In making an actual lace
you will be more usually working in diagonal lines
than in horizontal ones, but this offers no difficulty.

We can now start to make the first form of the
insertion. Hang two pairs at A, two at F, two at
K, and one each at B, C, D, E, G, H, I, J. With the
pair of B and one pair of A make the margin at 1. With

the pair of C and the right-hand pair of 1, Torchon-stitch at 2 ; then the margin at 3. With the pair of D and one pair of 2, Torchon-stitch at 4 ; with the left-hand of 4 and the right-hand of 3, Torchon-stitch at 5 ; then the margin at 6. In the same way, taking up the pair of E, Torchon-stitch at 7, 8, 9, and the margin at 10. Work the opposite side of the insertion in exactly the same way, taking the holes in the order indicated by the numbers.

Now make the lozenge of half-stitch. With the left pair of F and the pair of 7 (the latter twisted *twice*), h.s. and pin 21, then back, making h.s. with these two, the other pair of F, and take in the pair of 17, twisted twice ; set pin 22, and continue thus in the direction indicated by the zigzag line in the diagram. At pins 21–28 a new pair, twisted twice, is taken in, and those taken in at 2′ and 28 are left off again ; a pair is also left off at each of pins 29–34. On finishing the half-stitch below 35, repeat as from 1.

Second form.

Turn to the directions on page 88 for cloth-stitch, and practise it till you are sure of being able to make it accurately. Then make the insertion as before, only substituting cloth-stitches for the half-stitches in the lozenge.

Third form.—Spider.

When you are familiar with the second form of the insertion, you can proceed to work the final form, introducing the "spider," which is really only an adaptation of cloth-stitch. On completing a lozenge of cloth-stitch, as at 35, work the Torchon-stitches and marginal stitches on both sides, in the order of the numbers, from 36 to 65. Now make the "spider' thus : Twist three times each the pairs of 46, 47, 48, 61, 62, 63. Take the pair of 61, work cloth-stitch through pairs 46, 47, 48 ; set no pin, but hang up 61 temporarily. Take the pair of 62 and work cloth-stitch through the same three pairs as before, and hang up 62 likewise ; do the same with 63. Now set a pin at 66 so that three pairs fall on each side of it (pairs from 61, 62, 63 on the left, pairs from 46, 47, 48 on the right of the pin), take out the pin on which pairs from 61 and 62 were temporarily hung, and draw all the threads tight. This completes half the spider. The other half is worked just the same way : take the pair nearest the pin on the right, work cloth-stitch through the three pairs on the left, and similarly with the other two right-hand pairs. Again draw the threads tight, and twist each of the six pairs thrice, which completes the spider. Go on with the Torchon-stitches on both sides as before, in the order of the numbers, taking in the pairs from the spiders as indicated.

Note that a spider may be made with four pairs or eight as well as six ; the mode of working is the same in all cases.

No. 13.—*Cornered Lace*

This narrow lace with its angle would serve to edge a simple handkerchief or trim the revers of a chemise. If used together with the insertion to

match (No. 14), it would make pretty little tray-cloths
and d'oyleys, mats for a dressing-table, etc.

Hang on one pair of bobbins wound pair-wise[1]
at each point from B to I, three at A and two at K ;
—thirteen in all.   Mecklenburg thread No. 10.   Start
at A, twist the two left pairs twice, and then make
h.s. at 1 ; at 2 take in the third pair of A and the
pair from B, twisted twice, and continue h.s.   At 3
twist the outer pair twice as in lace No. 11, and always
do this where your outer edge is formed of h.s. ; it
gives greater firmness.   At 4, 6, and 8 take in the

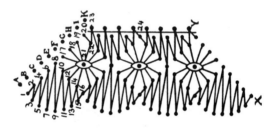

pairs from C, D, E in turn, each twisted twice.   At 8,
10, 12, 14, hang your extreme right-hand pair out of
the way, so that at 16 only three pairs remain.

Start again with the pair left at 8, make Torchon-
stitch down 17, 18, 19, 20.   Then form a spider with
the pairs hanging from 10, 12, 14, 17, 18, and 19.
From 20 to 22 h.s., take in the first leg of the spider ;
at 23 the two pairs from K, twisted twice.   Form
with them the straight margin as in lace No. 11.
Note that this is only done every second time that
you come to the edge ; the alternate times, the two
marginal pairs are left hanging, and the h.s. work

1 See above, p. 134.

simply returns from right to left. At point 24, when you will have completed one repeat of the pattern, return to 16.

To turn the corner. Work on like this until the straight edge is the right length for the cloth you wish to trim, then on again until you reach the points along the diagonal line X Y. With the left pair of the point next to Y, Torchon-stitches with the three pairs of the spider at the next three points along the diagonal line; the left pair of the last of these Torchon-stitches is taken into the h.s. of the scallop at its lowest point and immediately left off again. Thus you have the pairs arranged again as on the line A K; three pairs hanging at X, two at Y, and one at each intermediate point. Take out all your pins but those along X Y; gently pull the lace well up toward the heads of these remaining pins, and with care not to let fall any pins nor to tangle the bobbins, lift the whole fabric up from the pattern. Turn it so that you can set the pin from point Y at K, and all the others in order along the line to A. This requires some dexterity; a little tangling of the bobbins does not matter, but try to avoid any strain on the fabric which has so few pins to keep it in shape.

Corners may in this way be formed for almost all Torchons. Observe that the pins are set one row further back on being shifted.

Finishing off. Having turned the third corner and finished the last side, cut off all the bobbins, leaving about three inches of thread to the lace. Take out all the pins and hold the lace loose in your hand.

With a needle pass one thread of each pair through the corresponding loop left at the beginning, and knot it firmly to its fellow, either by a reefer or a weaver's knot. Cut off the ends neatly, but not too close to the knots for fear of their slipping.

No. 14.—*Insertion to match No. 13.*

This insertion needs no further explanation. It requires the same number of bobbins. Hang three pair at A, two at K, and one each at every other letter. Take the three pairs of A to form the margin

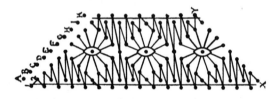

at 1, and then with the right of these three start the h.s. triangle. At the corner work to the diagonal line X Y and shift back these points, as in the edging, to the points A, K.

No. 15.—*Lace with Corner*

This lace, though differing a good deal from the ordinary Torchon patterns, may yet fairly be included in this chapter, since it has " Torchon-ground " and a geometrical pattern. Its lightness and openness have a very pleasing effect, and the design is not at all banal; moreover, it is fairly quickly worked. Seventeen pairs of bobbins are required with Mecklenburg thread No. 6. Hang two pairs at A, two at G, two at M, and one each at the other points marked by a letter. Twist the pair of F, take it c.s. through the pair of E (twisted), twist the workers, c.s. with the pair of D (twisted) and set pin 1; back in the same way to 2. From 2, take the workers as before through the pairs of E and D, twist them

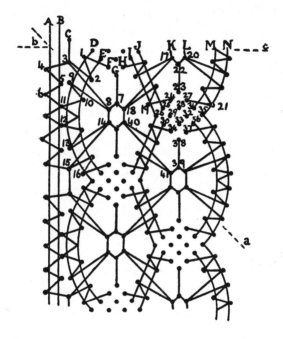

again, twist the pair of C three times, c.s. and pin 3, c.s. below the pin. Twist the left pair, take it c.s. through the pair of B twisted; twist the workers, and with the two pairs of A make the margin-stitch at 4; work back to 5 and to 6 in the same way.

Plait (see p. 95) the two pairs of G, set pin 7. Take the pair left below pin 3, c.s. through the pairs from D and E, twist it three times; twist also the left pair of 7, c.s. with these two at 8, and c.s. below the pin. Twist the left pair three times, and back as before to 9, thence to 10. From 10 work back through the two passives, and from 6 through the pair of B; with the workers of the margin and the workers of the scallop, c.s. at 11. From 11, take the right pair through the passives from D in the usual way, twist and make a c.s. with the inner pair of passives, but do not set a pin; the right pair of this c.s. become the passives; the left become the workers, and are taken back to 12, where they combine as at 11 with the workers of the margin. Work on in the same way to 13; from 13, the workers after passing through the passives are twisted thrice, c.s. at 14 with the pair of 8 twisted; twist the workers thrice again and continue the scallop. Work the margin as far as 15; here c.s. with the workers of the margin and the workers of the scallop. Continue the scallop up to 16; take the workers through the two passive pairs, and hang them up for the present.

Begin the next band at H, I, J; the pair of H are the workers, I and J the passives. It is worked like the scallop, the passive pairs being twisted each time, and the workers twisted between the passives. At 17 the workers, twisted thrice, make a c.s. with the pair of K twisted; at 18, also twisted thrice, they make a c.s. with the right pair of 7 twisted. Work to 19, take them back through the passives, and leave them hanging.

Now work the outer scallop, one pair of M being

the workers, the other and the pair of N being the passives. It is worked in just the same way as the inner scallop; at 20, the workers, twisted thrice, combine with the pair of L twisted. Work to 21 and back through the passives, and leave the workers hanging.

Twist the pairs of 20 and 17, c.s. and pin 22, plait to 23. Now you can make the diamond of Torchon ground. With the workers from 19 and the left pair of 23, Torchon-stitch at 24; with the left pair of 24 and the passives coming from J, Torchon-stitch at 25; with the left pair of 25 and the passives coming from I, Torchon-stitch at 26; hang up the left pair of 26, which will be one pair of passives in the next band. With the right pair of 23 and the workers coming from 21, Torchon-stitch at 27 ; other Torchon-stitches at 28, 29, 30; hang up the left pair of 30, which will be the second pair of passives in the next band. With the pair of 27 and the passives coming from M, Torchon-stitch at 31, and so on to 34; the left pair of 34 will be the workers in the new band. With the pair of 31 and the passives from N, Torchon-stitch at 35, and so on to 38. The pairs of 35 and 36 will be the passives for the next scallop, the pair of 37 the workers; the two pairs of 38 are plaited to 39.

Next work the band from 26 and 30 as before, not forgetting to connect with the pair of 18 at 40 and with the left pair of 39 at 41. After that the second diamond of Torchon-ground, and then the second scallop on the left, noting that the pair from 15 is twisted thrice, combined with the workers of the second scallop, and taken back to the margin as before.

These directions sound more complicated than the working really is ; the diagram makes the movement of the workers and passives perfectly clear. You have only to remember the twistings, which give the lace its pretty open effect.

In chapter IV. we have shown how to design a

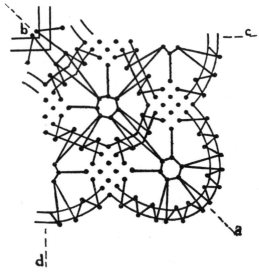

corner for this lace. Trace the corner on a separate piece of tracing-cloth. When you have worked to the line c b, pin the corner-pattern on the pillow, placing beneath it a piece of stiff felt or thick cardboard. Let one of the pins fastening the pattern and felt to the pillow be just inside the angle of the straight edge. As you work the corner, set the pins through the felt, but not into the cushion. When the corner is done, take out the pins that fasten the

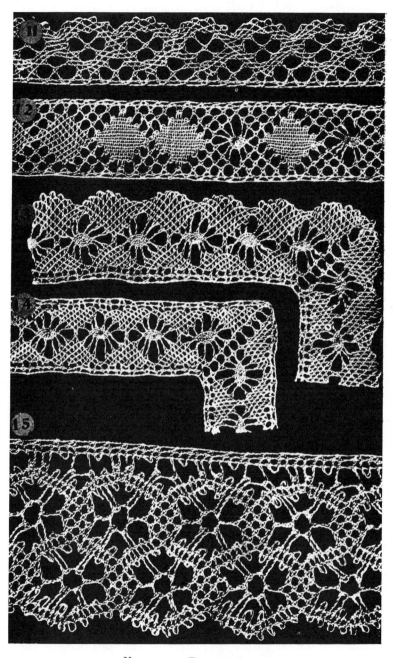

Nos. 11–15. Torchon Laces

pattern and felt down to the pillow, except the one in the angle ; turn the felt (with the pins of the pattern sticking in it) on this as a pivot till the line b d comes into the position formerly occupied by b c. The lace is now in the right position on the pillow for working the second side of the square.

It is perfectly simple to make an insertion to match this lace. If you omit the border (i.e. the pairs of A, B, and C), you get an insertion with two scalloped edges. If an insertion with two straight edges is desired you have only to add the border on the right side also. A corner may be made for the insertion in the same way as for the lace.

No. 16.—*Fringed Lace*

The scallops of this lace form a "fan," and in connection with it we give a simple and ingenious way of making a fringe, which may be used with any lace having a "fan" border. The fringe may, of course, be omitted, and as the "fan" is new to our readers, we shall first describe the method of working the lace without the fringe.

Seventeen pairs are required, wound with D.M.C. thread No. 30 ; if you intend to make the fringe, one pair may be wound with a coarser thread, e.g. D.M.C. No. 20, or even, if liked, with a coloured thread. Hang three at A, two at B, one at C, six at D, one at E, two at F, two at G (one of these being the fringe pair).

With the pair of C and one of D, both twisted,

c.s. and pin 1, c.s. below the pin; with the right
pair of 1 and the second of D (both twisted), pin 2;
with the right pair of 2 and the third of D, pin 3.
Begin again with the pair of E, and work it in the same
way through the other three pairs of D, setting pins
4, 5, 6, and remembering to twist both pairs each

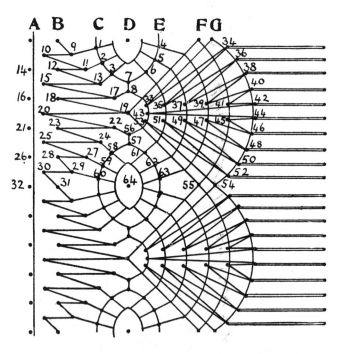

time. With the right pair of 3 and the left of 6,
c.s. and pin 7; then make these two pairs into a
plait (p. 95) long enough to reach to 8; set a pin at 8,
c.s. below it.

Take the pairs of F and 4, both twisted, make a
c.s., but set no pin; hang up the pair of 4 (the right-
hand pair of this c.s.), and take the pair of F in the

same way in succession through the pairs of 5, 6, and
the right pair of 8, twisting both pairs each time.
When you have made the last c.s. (with the pairs of F
and one of 8), leave both pairs hanging for the
present.

Work the triangle of half-stitch, beginning at B.
H.s. with the two pairs of B and the pair of 1, pin 9;
back to 10, here take in one pair of A and leave it off
again; back to 11, taking in the pair of 2; thence to
12 and to 13, taking in the pair of 3. Leave the pairs
of the half-stitches, and make the margin stitch at 14
in the usual way, with the pair left off at 10 and the
two pairs of A. Then resume the half-stitches from
13 to 15, taking in at 15 one pair of 14, and leaving it
off again, to be taken into the margin at 16. The
half-stitch triangle is continued in the same way; at
every alternate pin on the left side a pair is taken in
from the margin and left off again. At 17 take in the
left pair of 8; at 19 take in the pair that came from F,
and leave it off again; leave off a pair at each
succeeding pin on the right of the triangle.

Now make the fan. Take one pair of G (if you
have wound a coarse pair for the fringe, it is the
one to take); twist it and the pair hanging from F,
c.s., but no pin; take the workers (the pair coming
from G) in the same way in succession through
the pairs coming from 4, 5, 6, and 8, set pin 33;
c.s. and hang up the left pair. Take the workers
back in the same way through the remaining
passives, i.e. the pairs from 6, 5, 4, F, and
the other pair of G (remembering always to twist

both pairs), set pin 34. Work back through these
five passive pairs to 35, c.s. below the pin, and hang
the left pair up. Continue thus, taking the pins in
the order of the numbers, and leaving off a pair
below each of the pins 37, 39, so that you have one
passive pair less each time. From 42, go back
through all six passives to 43, and return to 44.
From 44, as the diagram clearly shows, you keep
taking up an additional passive pair each time, at
pins 45, 47, 49, 51, 53, when you have the whole six
taken in. On making the c.s. below 54, hang up
these two pairs. Take the pair left off at 19 in the
same way through the first *five* passives of the fan,
pin 55, c.s., and hang these two up.

Take the pair of 22 and the first passive of the
fan, twist, c.s., and pin 56 ; plait these two pairs to
57, c.s. below the pin. With the left pair of 57 and
the pair left off at 24 (both twisted), c.s. and pin 58 ;
similarly 59 and 60 with pairs from 27 and 29. In
the same way take the right pair of 57 through the
next three passives of the fan, setting pins 61, 62, 63.
Now work the spider with the six pairs from 58, 59,
60, 61, 62, 63 ; on completing the spider, repeat as
from the beginning.

To make the fringe. The fringe may be of any
desired length. In the diagram we have put the
dots near the fan to save space ; but the worker
has only to rule a line along her pattern at whatever
distance she likes, and set her pins on it. When the
workers of the fan reach 34, instead of making a c.s.
below 34, take the workers round a pin set at the first

dot of the outer row, and back; twist the passives at
34 again, c.s., and set an extra pin below this c.s.
(between 34 and 36) to keep the fringe in position,
and work to 37 as before. Each time that you
reach the edge the workers are similarly taken round
one of the outer pins. In the middle of the fan it is
not necessary to put an extra pin when the workers
are brought back to the edge, but only at the sides of
the fan, where the lines diverge widely; at points 46
to 54 the pins should be set *above* the cloth-stitches.

The fringe bobbins should be wound as full as
possible, as the thread is soon used up; when the
thread has to be joined, let the join be at the end of
the fringe. When the lace is finished, you have only
to cut the loops of the fringe.

No. 17.—*Lace*

This pretty lace requires twenty-one pairs of bobbins, which should be wound with D.M.C. thread
No. 35. Hang three pairs at A, three at B, five
at C, four at D, two at E, F, and G. With the
right-hand pair of B, work cloth-stitch through the
other two pairs of B, all six pairs of C, and one pair
of D; set pin 1. Return to 2, leaving off two pairs
at B; leave two pairs at 2. At 3 take up the second
pair of D, and leave it off again; at 4 leave off a pair,
also at 5 and 6. At 7 you will have two pairs left, of
which one is taken into the spider.

Now proceed to work the scallop. With two pairs
of A, make a plait to reach to 9. Take the third pair

of A, twist it, twist one pair of B, and make a cloth-stitch with these two pairs. Twist the workers and the second pair of B, make a cloth-stitch. In the same way, work through the pairs left off at 2 and at 4, each time twisting both the workers and the pair taken up. Set pin 8 and leave off a pair. Work back in exactly the same way through the remaining four passive pairs; twist the workers; cloth-stitch through one pair of the plait, set pin 9. Return

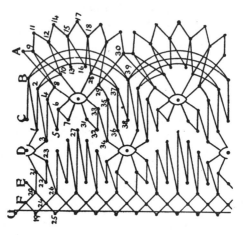

through the pair of the plait, twist the workers, and continue as before to 10; here leave off a pair. Take the pairs of the plait and work a plait to 11, set a pin; continue the plait to reach to 12, where it will be combined with the workers coming from 10. The rest of the scallop is worked in the same way; continue it to 18, then hang up all the pairs you have been using for the present. Begin now at the opposite edge of the lace. Make the margin at 19 with the pairs of G and one of F. Work half-stitches with

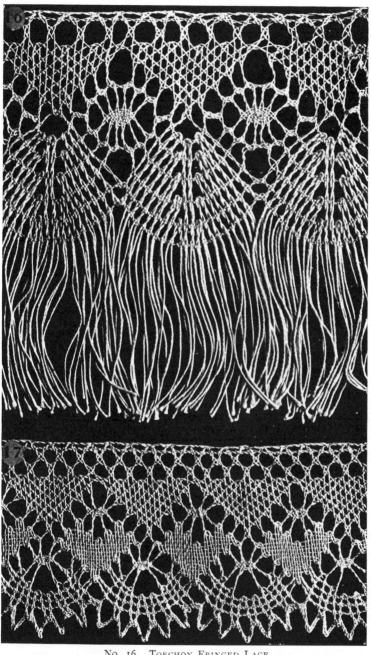

No. 16.   Torchon Fringed Lace
No. 17.   Torchon Lace

the pairs of E and the other of F, set pin 20, leave off
a pair.   Half-stitches to 21, taking in one pair of D,
thence to 22, thence to 23, taking in the other pair of
D.   At 24, Torchon-stitch with one pair from 19 and
one from 20 ; margin at 25.   Continue the half-stitches
from 23 to 26, taking in a pair from 24 ; below 26
leave off a pair.   Continue the triangle of half-stitches
as indicated in the diagram.   At alternate pins on
the left side of the triangle you will be taking in pairs
from the Torchon stitches and dropping them again.
On the right side of the triangle, the pairs from 3, 5,
and 7 will be taken in in succession, and after
reaching the apex of the triangle at 27, a pair must
be left off at each pin on the right.   When this
triangle is finished, make a spider with the pairs from
6, 7, 8, 10.   On completing the spider, you can finish
the scallop of the border, taking in pairs from the
spider at 28 and 29, remembering always to twist
both the passives and the workers before each cloth-
stitch.   Work to 30, make the plait from 30 and leave
the pairs you have been using aside.

Now work the heart-shaped *motif* of cloth-stitch.
Take the first left-hand pair of the spider, work cloth-
stitch with the pair left off at 27 (twisted) ; set pin 31.
Continue the cloth-stitches as the diagram shows ;
take in one pair at 32, 33, 34, 35, two at 37.   Work
the second spider.   From 39 repeat as from B, and
from 30 as from A.

No. 18.—*Insertion*

This insertion presents no new difficulty and needs little explanation. Wind twenty-six pairs with Mecklenburg thread No. 8; hang three at A, one each at B—J, two at K, one each L—T, and three at U. The joinings of the bands of cloth-stitch which separate the spiders are rather confusing: follow the lines in the pattern carefully. Make cloth-stitch with the

two pairs of K, take in the pair of L, and set pin 1; leave off a pair. Return to 2, taking in the pair of J; thence to 3; leave off a pair at 3, and work to 4, taking in the pair of I. Take the pair left at 3, and work cloth-stitch through the pair left at 1, and the pair of M; set pin 5. Below the spiders, the diagonal bands are connected as in lace No. 11, i.e. the workers from each side (6, 7) are combined by a cloth-stitch at 8.

No. 19.—*Lace*

This lace is similar to the insertion No. 18, and
the two can be used together for trimming tea-cloths,
etc. Twenty-four pairs are required. Hang three
at A, one each at B—J, three at K, three at L, six at
M. The mode of working is the same as No. 18.
Starting from K, work down the right-hand band of
cloth-stitch ; take the right pair of M as workers

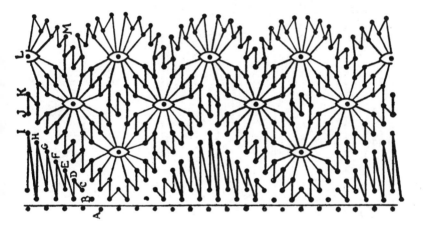

through the other five, and combine in the usual way
with the workers from K ; and so on as in No. 18.
Note that in working the spiders in the middle of the
scallop, the third leg on the right is formed by the
workers of the cloth-stitch of the scallop, and that
the pair which forms the fourth leg becomes in its
turn the workers of the scallop. Both this lace and
No. 18 may have the diagonal bands in h.s. if
preferred.

No. 20.—*Lace*

The model is a moderately heavy lace, worked with Mecklenburg thread No. 8.   It also makes a charming fine lace if worked with No. 50.

The squares on the pattern represent a stitch new to our readers—*rose-stitch*—which makes an excellent light filling for a large surface, or even the whole

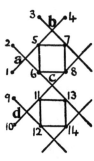

FIG. 40

grounding of a lace.   The Germans call it "violet-stitch," and the French "maiden's grounding."   The small diagram shows the method of working.   Hang a pair at 1, 2, 3, 4, 9, 10.   Combine the pairs of 1 and 2 by a whole stitch at *a*, but without setting a pin. Combine similarly at *b* the pairs of 3 and 4.   Now take the right-hand pair of *a* and the left-hand of *b*, make h.s. and set pin 5 ; h.s. below the pin.   Similarly, take the remaining pair of *a* and the left-hand of

5, h.s., pin 6 ; take the right-hand of 5 and remaining pair of *b*, h.s., pin 7 ; take the right-hand pair of 6 and left-hand of 7, h.s., pin 8. Now take the remaining pair of 6 and left-hand of 8, make a whole-stitch at *c* without setting a pin ; similarly, combine the remaining pairs of 7 and 8 by a whole-stitch. The next rose-stitch is now worked the same way : whole-stitch at *d* with the pairs of 9 and 10 ; h.s. at 11 with right pair of *d* and left of *c* ; h.s. at 12 with left of *d* and left of 11 ; h.s. at 13 with right of *c* and right of 11 ; h.s. at 14 with right of 12 and left of 13 ; finally, as before, a whole-stitch with pair of 12 and left of 14, and a whole-stitch with 13 and right of 14.

To work the lace thirty-two pairs are required. Hang three at A, one each at pins B to G, two at H, one each at I to N, two at O, one at P, one at Q, eight at R, three at S. Make the rose-stitch (as shown by the little diamond in the diagram) with one pair of A and the pairs of B, C, and D, and similarly with the other pairs up to the left-hand pair of O. Take the pair of Q, work h.s. through the eight pairs of R and one pair of S, set pin 1, leave off a pair ; with the left pair of 1 and the next pair on the left, h.s. and set pin 2, leave off a pair ; with the left pair of 2 work back to 3, taking in the pair of P. Continue to work the h.s. band as far as 7, leaving off a pair at each pin on the right, except at 6, where two must be left off, and taking in one at each pin on the left.

Now work the scallop just as described in No. 17, only that here the workers are not twisted between the three innermost pairs of passives (the pair from 5

and two pairs from 6).   Some care is required to make
the passives lie in graceful curves.   The spider is
worked as in No. 19.   On reaching 9 return to 7 and
work the h.s. band as indicated, taking in the left-
hand pairs of the spider and the passives of the scallop (remembering to take in *two* of these at 8), and
leaving off a pair at each pin on the left.   You can
now work the rose-ground up to the lozenge of cloth-
stitch, and next the lozenge itself, then repeat from
the beginning.

Nos. 18-20.   Torchon Laces

NOS. 21 TO 25. MALTESE LACES

CHAPTER IX

MALTESE AND CLUNY LACE

Yon Cottager, who weaves at her own door,
Pillow and bobbins all her little store;
Content, though mean, and cheerful if not gay,
Shuffling the threads about the livelong day,
Just earns a scanty pittance, and at night
Lies down secure, her heart and pocket light.
WM. COWPER ("Truth").

THIS lace accommodates itself even less easily to the hard and fast lines of a definition than does Torchon. One or two things are, however, certain about it; it is a guipure,[1] its designs are always geometrical and generally light, for the mats or solid figures of the design commonly occupy but a small proportion of the surface of the lace. This makes Maltese shade away from guipures into the class of plaited laces. Indeed, some of those in the following chapter might change places with some in this, but on the whole a glance will show that, important as is the rôle of the plait in Maltese lace, it is not all-important as in the laces of chapter x.

Maltese lace was, of course, originally supposed to come from Malta,[2] but for very many years a great deal of it has been made in Buckinghamshire and Nottingham. The term "Cluny" was never used in

[1] See p. 84.   [2] See p. 21.

this way ; it referred originally to copies of old lace in
the Musée Cluny at Paris, made mostly at Mirecourt,
in the Vosges district.   A great deal of Le Puy lace
is practically the same as Cluny.

The difference between Maltese and Cluny patterns
consists only in a nuance of style and in the relative
coarseness of thread used for the latter.   The sign
of "genuine Maltese" is supposed to be the Maltese
Cross, of which we give a specimen in No. 30.
Another typical characteristic is that it is very often
worked in silk, cream or black.   Buckingham Maltese
is most often worked in fine cotton, and Cluny always
in heavy linen thread, but such differences do not
touch the root of the matter.

Had it seemed possible to carry out a really scientific classification in laces, we would have called this
chapter "Geometrical Guipures" ; but as scientific
accuracy has not yet laid claim to our subject, we will
be content with the more familiar and vivid name as
it stands.

No. 21.—Narrow Lace

Wind eight pair of bobbins with Mecklenburg
thread No. 10.   Hang two pair at A, four at B, two
at C.   Take the left-hand pair of B, twist it twice,
and with the pairs of C make the margin‐stitch
(p. 118) at 1.   Take the left-hand pair of A, twist
it twice, work it in cloth-stitch (p. 88) through the
remaining three pairs of B ; also through the right-
hand pair of C twisted twice (p. 90), and set pin 2.
Make a cloth-stitch below the pin, hang up the left-

hand pair ; with the right, return cloth-stitch through
three pairs, twist the workers twice, and with the
remaining pair of A, twisted once, make a cloth-stitch,
and set pin 3 ; make a cloth-stitch below the pin.
Twist the left pair twice, cloth-stitch through three
pairs, and set pin 4. A cloth-stitch below the pin ;
hang up the left-hand pair, and return c.s. through
two pairs ; twist the workers twice, and with the pair
of 3 twisted once make a cloth-stitch, and set pin 5.
Continue to work the scallop in the same way as far
as 9 in the order of the numbers (only do *not* hang
up a pair at 6 or 8).

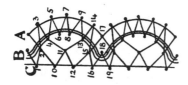

With the pair left off at 2, make margin-stitch at
10. With the right-hand pair of 10, and the pair left
off at 4, each twisted twice, make cloth-stitch, and set
pin 11 ; cloth-stitch below the pin, twist both pairs
twice. With the left pair of 11 make the margin
at 12.

Starting again at 9, continue as before to 13, but
before setting pin 13 take in the right pair of 11.
Cloth-stitch below pin 13, and return as before to
14 ; then back again, and make a cloth-stitch at 15
with the right pair of 12. C.s. below the pin, and
with the left pair twisted once make the margin at
16 ; with the right pair of 15 return as before to 17.

Twist once the right pair of 16, work it cloth-stitch through the three pairs of the scallop, set pin 18; return c.s. through the same three pairs, twist the workers once, and make margin-stitch at 19.

Starting again at 17, repeat as from A.

No. 22.—Narrow Insertion

Hang three pairs at A and L, one each at B–K, or sixteen in all, using Mecklenburg thread No. 6. On referring to the diagram it will be seen that this pattern mainly consists of pairs interwoven so as to

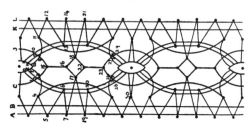

form intersecting curves or straight lines. Wherever the curves are shown crossing each other, the pairs are combined by a cloth-stitch, both being previously twisted once or oftener, according as the distance between the points is greater. It is not necessary to put a pin at all the crossings, but one may be put if you find it difficult to keep the lines in place; in any case, you must try to get the curves regular. Note that the only place where the threads are not twisted is in the bar of solid cloth-stitch from 6 to 20, and the corresponding one on the opposite side.

Take the pair of C, c.s. through the pairs of D, E, F, setting pins 1, 2, 3, then the pair of 3 through the pairs of 2 and 1, and the right pair of A through the pair of B; make a cloth-stitch with the pairs of A and the pair of 3, and set pin 4, cloth-stitch below the pin; with the left pair of 4, back through the pair of B to form the margin at 5, then take the right pair of 4 through the pairs of 1 and 2, and hang it up for the present. Take the right pair of 5 through the pair of B, then through the pairs from 1 and 2, *not* twisting it between them, and set pin 6. Take the left pair of 6 through the next pair on the left, twist it, and back to margin at 7. Leave this side, and work the other in the same way to 14. Combine the pairs left hanging from 3 and 8 at 15, make a plait (p. 95) to reach to 16, and set a pin. Take the right pair of 7, take it through the pair of B, twist it, through the two pairs of the cloth-stitch bar, twist again, and through the pair coming from 4, combine with the pair of 16, and set pin 17; return to the margin the same way at 19, back through the cloth-stitch bar, and set 20. Take the left pair of 20 through the other pair of the cloth-stitch bar and back to the margin. Continue as before, crossing the threads where shown, and work the other side of the insertion the same way. The pairs from 17 and 18 are twisted, cloth-stitch at 22, plait to 23. The pairs from 24, 25, 26, 27, 28, 29 form the spider (p. 123). When the spider is half finished, i.e. when you have set the pin, take the pair nearest the pin on the left through the other two left pairs, twist it, and take it (through the pair of the outer oval) to combine with a pair from the margin at 30 and back again through the same pairs;

do likewise on the other side with the pair nearest
the pin on the right, make a cloth-stitch with these
two pairs, take out the pin in the middle of the
spider and put it in again between these two pairs,
then complete the spider in the usual way, and repeat
from where you started.

No. 23.—*Edging to match No. 22*

Fourteen pairs are required : hang three at A, two
at K, one each at B—J. The centre and left side
of the pattern are worked in just the same way as
the insertion. For the scallop edging, proceed thus :

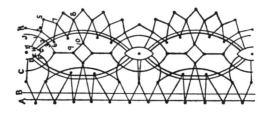

make with the two pairs of K a plait (p. 95) long
enough to reach to 4, twist the pair from 1, pass it
cloth-stitch through both pairs of the plait, set pin 4 ;
take the right-hand pair back through the other two
pairs, plait the latter, set pin 5, continue the plait till
it is long enough to reach to 7, leave it aside. Twist
the pair of 4, work it cloth-stitch through the pair of
2 (twisted) ; twist the workers and make a cloth-stitch
with the pair of 3 (twisted), and set pin 6. Take the
workers back as before through the pairs from 3 and
2, and at 7 work through the pairs of the plait as
you did at 4. Continue the scallop in the same way.

The workers from 3, after being taken through the two passive pairs, are twisted again and combined with the pair from 9 at 10, then brought back in the same way. On completing the scallop, the workers and the two passive pairs go to form the spider, while the plait is continued.

No. 24.—*Insertion*

Wind twenty pairs with Mecklenburg thread No. 10 ; hang two at A, four each at B and C, three each at F and E, two each at D and G.

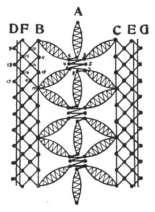

With the two pairs of A, two of B, and two of C make leaves (p. 95) long enough to reach to 1, 2, and 3 respectively. Set pin 1 between the two pairs of A, cloth-stitch below the pin, and cloth-stitch through the two pairs of B ; set pin 2. Return cloth-stitch through these three and the two pairs of C, set pin 3 ; cloth-stitch back to 4, 5, 6 ; at 6 leave off two pairs ; back to 7 and leave off two pairs ; with the two remaining pairs cloth-stitch and set pin 8.

With the two pairs of 6, 7, and 8 respectively make leaves as before.

The working of the borders is evident from the lines. With the two pairs of D, and the left pair of F twisted, make the margin at 9. With the right pair of F and one of B, each twisted, cloth-stitch and pin 10. With the right pair of 10 and remaining pair of B, each twisted, cloth-stitch and pin 11. Twist right pair of 9, cloth-stitch through the remaining pair of F and the left pair of 10, each twisted, and set pin 12. Take the left pair of 12, cloth-stitch through the pair coming from F (twisted); twist the workers and make the margin at 13. With the other pair of 12 and the left pair of 11, each twisted, cloth-stitch at 14, and so on. The other border is exactly the same. After making the cloth-stitch below pin 18, the right pair, twisted, is worked in cloth-stitch through the pair of 15 and both pairs of the leaf from 6; set 19, return cloth-stitch through the same three pairs, and then take the two right-hand pairs to make a leaf for the next flower.

No. 25.—Waved Lace

This lace makes a charming edging for a deep collar, the collar being cut in scallops to fit the scallops of the lace. It would also look well on brise-bise. Wind fifteen pair with D.M.C. thread No. 35. Hang two pair at A, B, C, D, three at E, two at F and G. The inner half of the lace is formed of two cloth-stitch braids, whose working presents no difficulty if the lines of the diagram are carefully followed. One pair of B forms the workers

of the first braid ; they are twisted between the other
pair of B and the nearest pair of A, but not between
the two pairs of A ; the passive pair of B is also
twisted each time. The pairs of C and D are
similarly worked. The workers of these two braids
are combined by a cloth-stitch at 1, 2, and similar
points indicated in the diagram.

With two pairs of E, make a leaf to reach to 3.
The workers of the second braid, coming from pin 2,

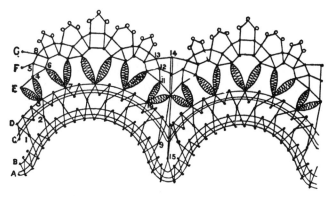

are to be passed c.s. through the two pairs of the
leaf ; set pin 3 ; take the workers back through these
two pairs, and continue the braid as before. With
the two pairs of 3 make a leaf to reach to 4 ; twist
the third pair of E and pass it c.s. through the pairs
of the leaf, and set pin 4 ; leave the left pair hanging, and make a plait with other two. Make also a
plait with the pairs of F. Taking the four pairs of
these two plaits, regard each pair as one bobbin,
make a cloth-stitch, and set pin 5 in the middle of
the stitch instead of below it. Take the two left-
hand pairs, plait them ; take up the pair left at 4,

twist and pass it c.s. through the pairs of the plait, and set pin 6; with the two pairs of the plait make a leaf to 7 (where they are combined as before with the workers of the braid) and another leaf back again.

Take the other two pairs of 5 and plait them; plait also the pairs of G, and combine these plaits by a c.s. at 8, as before, regarding each pair as one bobbin. Wherever the plaits are shown in the diagram as crossing, they are combined in this way. The diagram clearly shows where the plaits cross, where one of them is combined with the single pair that started from E, and where this pair in its turn is combined with the leaf pairs. The plait that forms the outer teeth of the scallop must have picots where indicated; these are made by setting a pin and twisting the thread of one bobbin of the plait round it.

The only other point that perhaps requires elucidation is the working at the middle point between the scallops. Twist the pair of 11 and take it through the pairs of the leaf from 10. The workers of the second braid coming from 9, after passing through the passives of the braid, are to be twisted three times, then passed c.s. through the pair of 11 and the leaf pairs from 10; then twist them twice, pass c.s. through the two pairs of the plait from 12; twist twice, pass c.s. through the pairs of the plait from 13, and set pin 14. Return in the same way (twisting the workers as before, but not the pairs coming from 13, 12, 11, and 10), and back through the braid to 15.

No. 26.—*Handkerchief Border*

Wind twenty pairs with Mecklenburg thread No. 10;
hang one at A, two at B, 4 at C, two at D, 6 at E,
one each at F—J. With two pairs of C, two of E,
and the two of D make leaves. Take one of the remaining pairs of C as workers for the border; c.s.
with the other pair of C, twist the workers, c.s. with
the two pairs of B, twist the workers and the pair of

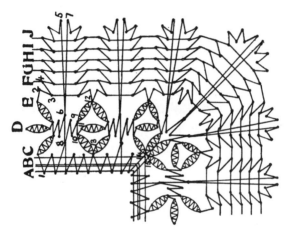

A, c.s. and pin 1; continue the border in the same
way.

Of the other four pairs of E take one as the
workers; make whole-stitches with the other three
in succession to 2; back to 3 in the same way,
leave off a pair; at 4 take in the pair of F, and so
on, leaving off a pair also at the five following pins
on the inside of the scallop, and taking in the pairs
from G—J (twisted) at successive pins on the outside
of the scallop. After 5, the workers are taken (still

in whole-stitches) through the passives of the scallop, then through the six pairs left off at 3 and the following pins; leave them hanging temporarily. With the pairs of the leaves from C, D, E work the cloth-stitches as shown as far as 6; here connect the workers with the workers from 5. Take the latter back in the same way as before in whole-stitches through the six pairs and the passives to 7, and continue the other side of the scallop, taking in pairs (twisted) at the pins on the inside, and leaving pairs off on the outside.

Continue the c.s. of the centre; at 8 connect with the workers of the margin. Two pairs at 9, 10, 11 are made into leaves; that from 9 is fastened in by the workers of the scallop at 12, that from 10 by the workers of the margin at 13, and the leaves from 11, 12, 13 go to form the next c.s. centre.

The corner presents no additional difficulty. After the workers of the margin have been connected with the leaf at 14, they are not taken back through the passives of the margin, but left hanging, until the third leaf comes back from the c.s. centre and is connected with them at 15, after which they are taken back through the passives in the usual way. In working the c.s. centre be careful not to pull the passives tight; they should lie in a curve. As at the corner the scallops are further apart, the outer pairs connecting one with another should be twisted twice.

No. 27.—Lace

This is a handsome heavy lace of the kind usually known in England as "Cluny." It requires twenty-seven pairs of bobbins, with Mecklenburg thread No. 6. Hang two pairs at A (one for the outer passives, one for the workers), one at B (passives), four at C (two to be the inner passives, the others for a plait), six at D (two for the flower, two each for the plaits on each side), two at E (for a plait), two at F (one the inner passives, one the workers), two at G (passives), four at H (for two plaits), two at I (for the outer plait).

This lace offers no difficulty to any one who has worked the preceding laces of this section. The intersecting plaits of the edge of the scallop are worked as in No. 25; the outer one has picots where shown; so have also the plaits from C, E, and the two from D encircling the flower. The flower requires two additional pairs; they should be hung on at pin 1 to make the middle leaf on that side (the workers of the margin being taken through them). The two pairs taken out of the c.s. centre at 2 to form the middle leaf on that side must be cut out at 3 after the workers have passed through them, and the ends neatly fastened. Between the flowers is a bar of c.s. made with six pairs; its workers are connected, as shown in the diagram, with the margin on one side and the scallop on the other.

Where two plaits intersect, this is done, as in No. 25, by a c.s. taking two bobbins as one; at the point

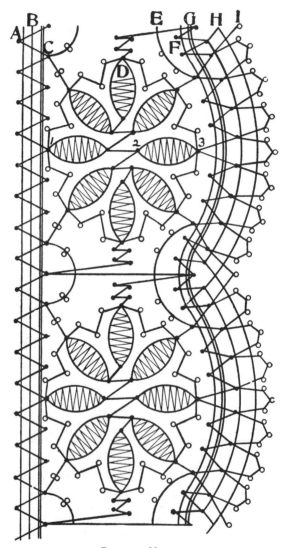

PATTERN No. 27

corresponding to D at the opposite side of the flower, make c.s. with four pairs taking two bobbins as one, and leave the two outer pairs to be taken afterwards into the c.s. band.

We have inserted this lace partly to introduce a way of working the petals with coloured thread, though they may of course be worked all white in the ordinary way. Choose a good washing thread; red or blue marking-cotton is very suitable, or coloured flax thread. When you have set the pin at the top of the leaf, take a needleful of the coloured thread and put the end of it over the pin, not knotting it, but turning the end down so that it is caught in the leaf. Now regard the two middle bobbins as one bobbin, and work the coloured thread in and out just as in the ordinary leaf you do one of the bobbins. If preferred, the coloured thread may be wound on a bobbin, but for finishing it off it is simpler to have a length of it threaded in a needle. When the leaf is the required length and neatly narrowed down to a point, slip the needle back under one or two of the threads, draw it tight, cut the thread off close to the surface of the leaf, and continue the working of the lace with the four bobbins.

If the flowers are thus worked with a coloured thread, the same thread might be used in the scallop; the bobbins forming any of the passives of the scallop might be wound with it.

PATTERN NO. 28

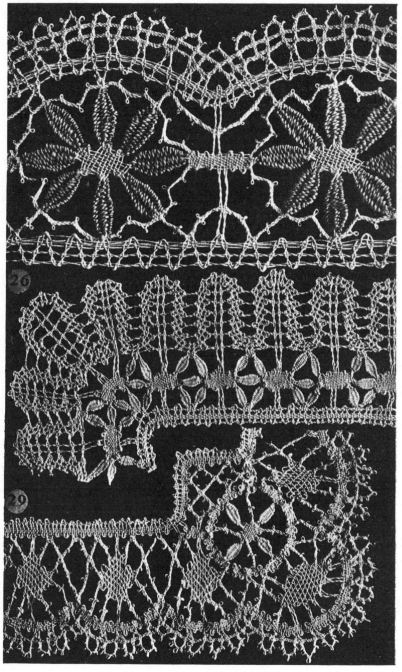

No. 27. Cluny Lace with Coloured Flowers
No. 26. Maltese Handkerchief Border
No. 29. Maltese Handkerchief Border

No. 28. Trimming for a Blouse (Maltese)

No. 28.—*Trimming for a Muslin Blouse*

The original model in the Museum at Plauen-im-Vogtland has the centres of the larger squares filled by a guipure pattern which necessitates the constant adding and cutting away of forty extra pairs. For this we have substituted embroidery in satin stitch worked in Moravian cotton on lawn. Cross-stitch on coarse linen might also be used, or fine darned net work, according to the material used for the blouse.

For the turnover collar of the blouse use only one side of the pattern; place the border point of the large square below the chin, and repeat the *edge* of the small square (without any of its centre) as often as the length of the collar-band requires. Of course, both the c.s. bands will in that case suffer no decrease in the number of their passives, and the connecting plait will go to and fro without alteration.

Turned-back cuffs may be treated in the same way with the large square set on to the front part of the wrist.

Thread Barbour's No. 80 (3-cord). Hang on eight pair at A, five at B, on either side, together twenty-six. Start the c.s. band at A, taking out a plait both to right and to left, one for the edging, the other to act as connecting link between the two c.s. bands on which the pattern is based. Each vandyke of the edge has a picot at the point; the large vandykes opposite the small square have three apiece. At 1 the connecting plait turns to a leaf, and after joining the corner band at 2 returns in a second leaf to the

outer band at 3. Here the two pairs must be
taken as passives into the c.s. of the outer band until
4 is reached. Then take a leaf back to 2, cross
the workers hanging there in c.s. with the left-hand
pair of the leaf, take out the pin, put it between the
two pair just crossed, and make the fourth leaf with
the old workers and the right-hand pair. Continue
the inner band with the left-hand pair from the leaf
as workers, making the "Russian" angle as described
on page 93.

At 5 the connecting plait goes out in a leaf again
to 6, then turns to a plait till 7 and joins the outer
band as a leaf at 8, is absorbed as passives in the
outer band till 9, when it returns again as a leaf to 7,
to which it is joined by a sewing (see p. 94) and
proceeds as a plait to 10.

Each side of the square is exactly alike. Work
down the left side to 12, set a pin there, letting the
workers fall to the left, the last pair of passives to the
right of it. Then resume the right side at 10. After
11 take the workers of the right across the passives as
usual, then twist them twice and continue across both
passives and workers of the left which were hanging
at 12. Take out the pin at 12, replace it between the
two pairs of workers and return with the workers of
the right, twisting them again just below the place
where they were twisted before. Just below 11
change them for the last pair of passives (as at
point 2) and continue these as workers.

At 13 the connecting plait is taken into the outer
band and two pairs brought out to join the inner

band one after the other. At 14, after touching the inner band the second of these pairs returns to 15, whence it and a pair from the outer band are taken to the inner as a plait. Now only three pairs remain to form the outer band, which becomes openwork, each pair being twisted twice before each crossing (as in the Russian braid, No. 9, p. 92). In like manner the inner band from 14 on. Take the pair joining the two bands across both pairs of the inner band hanging at 16 and out again. Twist the left pair at 16 twice and change it with the pair at 17, which become the workers.

Repeat all this on the opposite side. Then work the centre of the little square, which needs no explanation.

The lower sides of the little square are like the upper : take down a double plait from 18 to 19, after which point the outer band becomes c.s. again ; so does the inner band when the plait from the centre comes in below 20. Take back a single pair from 19 to 20, and at 21 let it enter the outer band as passive. At 22 bring in another pair from the inner band, and take both these pairs out again in the joining plait to 23.

No. 29.—Handkerchief Border

Worked with Mecklenburg thread No. 10, this would be suitable for a handkerchief border ; it might also be worked in coarser thread for toilet-table mats, etc. Nineteen pairs are required for the edging, and fourteen additional pairs for the corner. Trace the

section of the pattern *a...a* to *b...b* twice on strips of
tracing-cloth, to be put one below the other as many
times as are required for a side of the handkerchief,
and the corner section *b...b* to *c...c* on another piece.
As you begin to work the corner, a piece of felt or

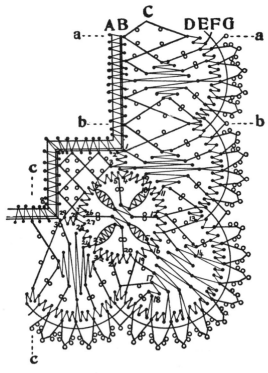

card should be slipped under the pattern, and the
pins stuck through it (see p. 130); when you come to
the middle of the corner, the felt can be turned round
on the pillow without disturbing the lace or pins, so
as to bring the next side of the handkerchief into the
proper position for working, and fastened down to
the pillow again.

Wind the bobbins pairwise; hang two pair each at
A, B, four at C, five at D, two at E, F, and G. Any
one who has worked the previous laces will need no
explanation for the edging; the diagram shows where
the plaits cross, or are caught in with the c.s. of the
scallops or the straight border, or taken into the
central lozenge, which is to be worked in half-stitch.
For the straight edge, the workers are twisted between
the pair of A and the nearest pair of B, but not
between the pairs of B.   The pairs of D form a solid
band of c.s. without twistings.

To work the corner.   At pin 1 hang on three pairs,
take the workers of the edge through them, set pin 2.
Continue the edge with the left pair below pin 2, and
the same passives as before. With the right pair of 2
as workers and the other two pairs hung on at 1,
make a c.s. band as indicated. At 3 hang on four
more pairs to form the plaits (taking the workers of
the c.s. through them). Continue the c.s. band to 4;
at 4 hang on three more pairs, and, as at 2, make the
left band with three pairs and the right with three.
Work the left band; at 5 and 6 hang on two pairs
each for the flower. Work this band to 7, and the
rest of the angle to 8; at 7 cut out the pairs of the
plait.

Return to 4 and work the right side of the circle
round the flower. At 9, 11, take in plaits from the
lozenge; at 10, 12, take out two pairs each for the
flower. Now work the flower, making leaves with
the pairs from 6 and 10, and plaits with picots with

the pairs from 5 and 12. Work the centre in c.s., and make leaves to 15 and 23, plaits to 20 and 26.

Begin working the corner scallop. At 13 hang on again the pairs cut out at 7 to form the plait (taking the workers through them as usual). Work the lozenge to 14; then go back to 12 and continue the circle, connecting with the plait from 13. At 15 take in the petal. At 16 leave off two pairs for a plait to the lozenge. Now continue the lozenge from 14, leaving off plaits where shown; at 18 cut out two pairs.

When the corner scallop is worked, continue the circle from 16. At 19 connect with the plait; at 20 take in the plait from the flower; at 21 take in the plait from the scallop, and at 22 leave off two pairs for a plait to the next lozenge; at 23 take in the petal, at 24 leave off two pairs, and again at 25, these latter two being cut out when they are taken into the lozenge.

Go back to 7, work to 26, take in the plait and cut it out. Take the workers from 27 through the three pairs of the other side to 28, cut out three pairs. Continue the c.s. with the other three pairs to 29; here take in the plait and cut it out. Go back to the margin and work from 8; at 30 take in the three pairs of 29 and cut them out, connect also with the plait from the lozenge. The additional pairs are now cut out again, and the working of the lace continues as before with the original 19.

Be sure you fasten the ends of the threads when you cut the bobbins off: in the case of the pairs cut off at 28 and 30, this is best done by darning each

thread with a needle through the c.s. bands for
a short distance, then cutting them off close ; in other
cases they may be tied together very neatly and cut
off short.   On completing the handkerchief, finish in
the usual way by knotting the ends through the loops
of thread at the beginning of the lace.

No. 30.—*Small Square*

This little medallion can be inserted in blouses,
collars, etc.   Wind thirty-three pairs with Mecklen-

burg thread No. 10; it is necessary to wind the
bobbins in pairs.   Hang four pairs at A, two at B.
Take the left pair of A through the other three, twist
it twice, make c.s. with the pairs of B, remove the pin
and set it in again below the c.s.; take the right pair
back again through the other two ; twist it.   Plait the
next two pairs of A to reach to 1, pass the workers

from B c.s. through both pairs of the plait, hang on
two more pairs at 1, and take the workers from B
through them likewise. Twist the workers, twist
the remaining pair of A twice, c.s. and pin 2. You
have four pairs at 1, the two middle ones are plaited
to 3, the right and left pairs are the inner passives of
the margin to right and left respectively. Twist the
workers from 2, twist the left pair of 1 twice, c.s. and
pin 4 ; continue this margin in the same way, hanging on two pairs at 5 and again at 6, till you come to
7, then leave this side.

Start again at B, twist the left of the two pairs
hanging at B and the remaining pair of 1 twice, c.s.
and pin 8 ; continue the margin in the same way,
hanging on two more pairs at 9, till you come to 10 ;
leave the margin.

Make leaves with the pairs hanging at 9, 3, 5, 6,
and work the flower as in No. 24. When the flower
is complete, start again the margin at 10 ; at 15 take
in the pairs of petal 11 ; at 16 take the workers c.s.
through all the pairs from 15 and back, leaving two off ;
at 17 hang on one more pair, and leave the margin.

Plait the pairs left off at 16 to 18, and proceed to
work the first section of the Maltese cross in c.s. in
the direction indicated in the diagram. Leave off the
right pair of 18. Hang two new pairs on a tem-
porary pin set between 18 and 19, take the left pair of
18 (the workers) through them and set 19. One pair
must be hung up at each of the pins 20, 22, 24, 26,
28, 30, two at 32, one each at 34, 36, 38, 40, 42, 44, 46.
On the other side hang on two new pairs at 21, two at

23; plait the pairs of petal 12 and take the plait in at 25; hang on two more pairs at 27 and two at 29; take in the pairs of petal 13 at 33; plait the pairs of 14 and take them in at 41. After 46 you will have two pairs left; plait them to 47, and here take them into the margin. Continue the margin (with all three pairs of 47 as passives); at 48 hang on a pair and leave it hanging; at 49 leave off two of the three passive pairs; at 50 leave the margin.

Twist the pairs hanging at 48 and 46, c.s. at 51; leave the left pair hanging; twist the right pair and the pair of 44, c.s. at 52, and so on down the middle of the cross to 57. Then twist the pair hung on at 17, and make cloth-stitches in the same way with the pairs left off at 20, etc. to 58.

Return to 49, plait the two pairs to 59 and take in the pair hanging at 51, and continue to work the second section of the Maltese cross, taking in pairs from 52 and 53, to 60; at 60 leave out two pairs.

Continue the margin from 50. At 61 hang on two new pairs, and again at 62, and hang them up as soon as the workers of the margin have been taken through them. Work to 63. Hang on two new pairs at 64, take the *passives* from 63 through them; plait them to 65; at 65, take the inner passives of the margin through the workers from 63 and through the pairs of the plait; plait the two right-hand of these four pairs to 66 and leave the other two hanging.

Plait the pairs from 60 to 67, and work the flower with the pairs from 67, 61, 62, 66. Next continue the cloth-stitches of the cross from 60, taking in pairs from 54, 55, 56, 57; at 72, take in the pairs of petal 68; at 73 leave off two pairs, and one at each succeeding pin on the right side of this section of the cross; plait the pairs of petal 69 and take them in at 75; of the three pairs left at 76, the right one is hung up, the other two plaited to 77.

Taking the left of the two pairs of 65 as workers, continue the margin; take in petals 71 and 70, and cut them out; at 77 take in the pairs of the plait from 76, and cut them out; at 78 leave the margin.

Return to the centre of the square; plait the pairs of 32 and the pairs of 73. Take these and also the pairs of 57 and 58 (twisted); you now have twelve bobbins in your hand; regard each three bobbins as one, and make a c.s. at 79. Take the two left-hand bobbins of 79, twist them and the pair left off at 74; c.s. at 80, and so on down that arm of the cross to 81; take one pair of 81 into the margin, and cut it out.

Now work the upper right-hand quarter of the square in the same way. Resume the margin at 17; at 82 hang on two pairs, plait them to 83 and work the section of the cross, taking in pairs at each pin on the left; at 84 leave off two pairs for the flower, and go back to the margin at 82. At 85, 86, hang on two pairs each; at 87 hang on two pairs, and work this corner just like the opposite one. Work the flower as before, then continue the section of the cross, taking in the petal pairs as shown and cutting them out; at 88 take in two pairs from 79 plaited; of the three pairs left at 89, one is hung up, the other two plaited and taken into the margin at 90. Work the margin from the corner, taking in the leaf-pairs and cutting them out.

Take the next pair of 79, work it as before down the middle in succession through the pairs left off from the cross to 91, and cut it out. Now work the last section of the cross from 93, taking in successively two pairs (plaited) from 92, the seven pairs from the line of pins between 79 and 91, the two remaining pairs of 79 plaited, and the seven pairs from the line of pins 80 to 81. Leave off two pairs each at 94, 95, 98; these, with two pairs hung on at 102, make the fourth flower. Above 96, 97, 99, 100, 101, cut out two pairs each from the middle of the c.s. passives. Plait the remaining pairs to 104, take them into the margin and cut them out; continue the margin, take in the two petals and cut them out. Work the other side from 102, take in a petal at 103, and cut it out; work both margins to the corner. At 105 cut out the inner passives and the workers from each side; plait the other two pairs, fasten them together with the outer passives at 106 and cut them out.

Note carefully the directions given on page 94 for hanging on additional bobbins, and remember, when you cut a pair out, to fasten the threads (having first taken the workers through them) by a knot as nearly invisible as possible. This is, however, not necessary in the case of the threads cut out above 96, 97, 99, 100, and 101, as being in the middle of a solid piece of cloth-stitch they do not tend to unravel, and may simply be cut off close.

No. 31.—*Square*

This little square may be used to insert in the corners of a tea or tray cloth, cushion slip, cradle cover, or, indeed, in an endless variety of ways that will suggest themselves to the ingenious worker. It

requires thirty-three pairs of bobbins wound in pairs with Mecklenburg thread No. 8.

Hang four pairs at A and combine them by a c.s., taking each pair as one bobbin; two pairs go on each side to form the margin of the square. This margin is slightly different from those already shown, and is

worked thus : Plait the two margin pairs ; take the
inner pair, twist it, make a c.s. with the workers of
the c.s. band also twisted ; then twist both pairs
of the margin, and continue the plait again.   Hang
six pairs at B.   Hang four pairs at C, and combine
them by a c.s., taking each pair as one ; the middle
two pairs will then be plaited ; the left-hand pair
will form the workers on the left, and is to be taken
through the three pairs hanging on the left of B,
and similarly the right-hand pair of C will be
taken through the three pairs hanging on the right
of B, and form the workers for the right-hand c.s.
band.

Work the margin on the left, hanging on two pairs
at 1, 2, 3, and four pairs at 4, to form plaits, till you
reach 5 ; leave this side and go back to the corner.
Work the right side, hanging on two pairs at 6 and 7
to form plaits, till you reach 8.   Now work the plaits
and circle.   The plaits from 1, C, 6 are combined by
c.s. at 9, taking three bobbins as one ; take one plait
from 9, and the plait from 2, c.s. at 10, taking two
bobbins as one ; with plaits from 10, 3, 4, c.s. at 11,
taking three bobbins as one ; 12 like 10.   Next work
the circle of c.s. in the middle with the pairs of the
plaits from 10, 9, 12, 11, as shown.   Complete the
circle in the same way, working round from 11 to 13
and from 12 to 13 ; at 13, c.s., taking three bobbins as
one.   Now continue the margin from 8 to 14, taking
in or leaving out pairs where shown.

After 14, cut off the two marginal pairs and the
nearest two pairs of passives, leaving three inches of

thread ; knot the threads together temporarily, and
pin the knot down out of the way outside the pattern.
Of the other four pairs of the braid, take the right
pair of workers through the other three to 15 ; back
to 16 and take in the plait ; at 17 leave off one pair.
Continue this c.s. band to 18, taking in and leaving
off pairs where indicated.

Set a pin at 19, hang on it one additional pair ; c.s.
with the pair of 17 (both twisted), set pin, and work
petal 20. Set another pin at the end of the petal
and plait the pairs. Work petal 21 ; c.s. (taking two
bobbins as one) with the plait from 20 ; hang up the
pairs of 21 and continue the plait ; similarly with
petals 22, 23 ; set pin 26 and turn the plait to the
left ; take petals 24 and 25 through it as before.
Work 27, set a pin at the end. Start the c.s. band
again at 18, take in a pair from 27 at 28, and the
plait at 29 ; at 30 connect with the workers of the
margin. Continue as far as 33, leaving off two
pairs at 31 and at 33, and taking in at 32 the other
pair of 27.

Work petals 34, 35, 36, and go on from 33, taking
in the petals and leaving off two pairs at 37, till you
come to 38. Return to the margin at 30, work to 43,
hanging on two additionals at 40, 41, 42. Work the
second circle like the first, then resume the margin
to 45.

From 39 continue the c.s. band, leaving off pairs
for the petals and taking in the plaits, and at 46
taking in three pairs from the margin. On reaching
47, work the petal and stem (as from 17) ; take the

No. 30. Small Maltese Square
No. 31. Maltese Square

No. 32. MALTESE LACE TIE

next petal through the stem at 48 as before. Work down the c.s. band, taking in petals 48 and 49. Leave off two pairs for the largest petal, work it, and fasten it by a "sewing" (p. 94) into the pinhole at 26, also the pairs of the stem.

Work the margin 46 to 50; here hang on two additional pairs. Work the plaits and circle as before, and the margin to 51.

Continue the c.s. band of the central figure, leaving off pairs for the petals. Work the plait for the stem from 26, and the petals as far as 52; resume the c.s. band, connecting with the margin at 53, down the next side to 54 (taking in the petals and leaving off pairs for the plaits). Margin to 55, then the fourth circle.

Return to 54 and continue the band, taking in petals on one side and plaits on the other. Each time you take in two pairs, cut out two pairs of passives in the middle of the c.s. so as not to have more than five. At 19 fasten the workers by a sewing into the loop of the pair hung on there.

Continue the margin from 55. On reaching 14, cut off the bobbins of the workers, leaving three inches of thread; thread one into the pinhole at 14, knot them very neatly, and cut off short; similarly with the workers of the central band when they reach 14.

Take out the pin which holds the knot previously made, undo the knot, tie the threads of the marginal pairs neatly together, and cut off short. Cut off all the other bobbins, take the square off the pillow, thread each hanging end in turn with a needle; darn it neatly for a quarter of an inch or more through the c.s. bands, then cut it off close.

This square looks better (though it is rather more complicated to work) if the marginal band is kept the same thickness throughout by cutting out passives from the middle whenever others are taken in, so that the number never exceeds three pair; they must be hung in again afterwards as required. This has been done in the specimen photographed.

No. 32.—Lace Tie.

This pretty and useful tie may be worked with Mecklenburg thread No. 10, or with lace silk. It takes forty pairs, and the bobbins must be wound in pairs. Trace the pattern once from the end to $a \ldots a$, and twice from $a \ldots a$ to $b \ldots b$. The latter section is repeated as often as is required to make the tie the proper length. A yard and a half is a frequent length, which would require twenty-nine repeats, besides the end pieces. This length allows for the tie encircling the neck twice as well as making a bow; if it is only wanted to go round once, eight repeats less would suffice.

Hang four pairs over a pin at A, twisting the four threads once round the pin; make a plait with the four bobbins that fall on the left of the pin, and a plait with the four on the right. Hang four pairs at B, and do the same with them. The left plait of A and the left plait of B make the margin on the left-

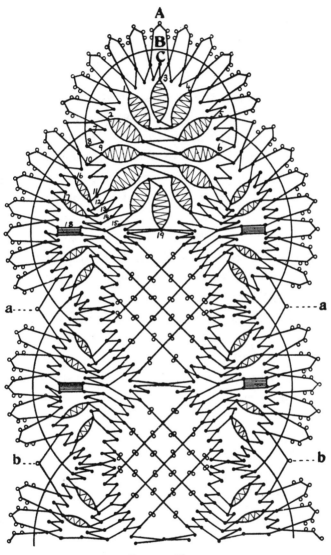

PATTERN No. 32

hand as shown in the diagram, and the other two
plaits the right-hand margin. At C hang twelve
pairs; with the 6 falling to the left of the pin, work the
c.s. braid on the left, and similarly with the others on
the right. At each of the points 1, 2, 3, 4, 5, 6, hang
on two pairs for the petals of the flower. Work
round the left side to 8 ; at 7 two pairs are left off to
make the inner plait of the next scallop, and at 8 two
pairs are taken in from the plait of the first scallop as
shown. Similarly on the right side ; work it to 6,
then work the flower. At 9 take in the pairs of the
petal, and hang on three pairs. You now have eleven
pairs ; work from 9 through four of these to 10 ; with
the right pair of 10 work back through the other
three to continue the c.s. band surrounding the
flower; with the left pair of 10 work through the
remaining six to make the c.s. band of the next
scallop. On the other side, *five* additionals must be
hung on instead of three, otherwise it is worked in
the same way ; after 6, four pairs go to the inner
band and seven to the outer. The middle of the
flower is worked in cloth-stitch, and the lozenges in
the scallops in half-stitch. On finishing the flower
the petals are taken into the cloth-stitch as indicated.
A pair is left out at 11, 12, 13, 14, 15, to be taken
into the lozenge, and two pairs each at 16 and 17 to
make the leaves. At 18 the workers of the c.s. braid
and of the lozenge are formed into a rectangular bar
(see p. 96). At 19 one pair of the petal is taken into
the c.s. band on the right, the other into the band on
the left, and the workers of the two bands are com-

bined in c.s. The ovals down the middle are filled in with plaits, crossing as shown, and ornamented with picots. The working of the rest is obvious.

On reaching the other end of the tie, the bobbins are cut out at the points corresponding to those where they were hung in ; the joins must be made very neatly.

CHAPTER X

PLAITED LACE

*Je m'avisai, pour ne pas vivre en sauvage, d'apprendre a faire des lacets.
Je portois mon coussin dans mes visites, ou j'allois comme les femmes travailler
à ma porte et causer avec les passants.   Cela me faisoit supporter l'inanite du
babillage, et passer mon temps sans ennui chez mes voisines.*

JEAN JACQUES ROUSSEAU, "Confessions"
(under 1762).

PLAITED lace is perhaps the earliest of all laces. We have seen[1] what an important part is played by plaited patterns in the oldest pattern-books.   The idea of reviving these old designs is very tempting, but it offers many difficulties, for the laces most in fashion in the sixteenth century do not at all fulfil our present requirements, especially in the matter of solidity.   We have, nevertheless, included Nos. 33 and 34 as specimens.

Plaiting, however, is bound to survive in laces in some form or other.   It is so necessary a development that every lace-making district offers some variety of plaited lace, hence, like Torchon, it bears no geographical name.   Our examples come from Saxony, Le Puy, and Russia.   Plenty of interesting specimens are to be found in Italy.   England has less of the kind to show, and that principally as a branch of "Maltese."[2]

[1] pp. 17, 26, etc.   [2] See p. 145.

The technique of plaited laces is very simple. Our reason for placing it towards the end of this book is that to make a good effect with such slight material considerable intricacy is needed. The material consisting, as it does, almost entirely of lines with no large solid figures, many lines must be introduced; this presupposes a fair number of bobbins, and the mazy designs are too puzzling for a beginner to follow easily.

The elements of plaited lace are plaits of two, three, and four pair; ornaments, of which the commonest are some form of leafwork; and footings of different kinds, preferably not plaited, as other footings offer greater firmness.

The ordinary *plait of two pair* is fully described on p. 95.

The *plait of three pair* is formed like a common hair-plait, each pair being taken as one thread.

To form a *plait of four pair*, make c.s. with the right pair of the left plait and the left pair of the right plait, and set a pin between them at the point where the two plaits are to unite to form the plait of four. Then c.s. with the remaining two pairs *over* the pair of the first set which falls between them. Resume the first set, c.s. *over* a pair of the second set, and so on, forming each plait alternately over a pair of the other.

Neither of the two latter forms of plait are used for their own sake. At best they are a shade clumsy in comparison with the first; but the construction of the lace may require them.

The next essential of plaited lace after the working
of the plaits themselves is the formation of their *intersections*.   That of two plaits is made by a single
c.s., in which each pair plays the part of a single
thread.   That of three plaits is made by a c.s., in
which three bobbins are taken as one.   Other intersections are comparatively rare.

The ornaments used to break the monotony of the
plaits are most often leaves, flowers, and stars of
barwork (p. 96), because the same number of bobbins is required for these as for a simple plait.
Lozenges and other figures in c.s. and h.s. are also
used, especially at points where a number of plaits
come together.

No. 33.—Lace

We give here a very charming edging taken from
Le Pompe (see p. 17).   We have added, to give it

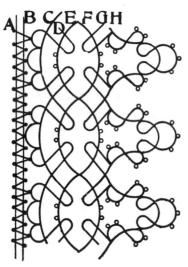

greater firmness, a simple
footing (two pairs of passives, twisted each time,
and the workers twisted
between them).   Wind fifteen pairs with Mecklen-
burg thread No. 6; hang
two at A, one at B (these
for the footing), two each
at C, D, E, F, G, H for
the plaits.   The working
is quite obvious, the diagram showing sufficiently

where the plaits cross. The only difficulty is in
shaping the curves well. In some places the picots
enable this to be done; in other places (e.g. in
the four loops in the centres of the ovals) we have
found it useful to set several pins on the inside of the
curve to keep it in shape. Pins may also be set, if
you find it of assistance, wherever the plaits intersect,
though we have not thought it necessary to indicate
these pins in the diagram.

No. 34.—*Insertion*

This insertion is likewise taken from Le Pompe,
with the addition of a footing (as in No. 33) to make

it firmer. It is a good deal
similar in character to the
edging. Wind eighteen pairs
with Mecklenburg thread No.
6, hang two at A, one at B
(for the left margin), two
each at C, D, E, F, G, H
(for the plaits), one at I, two
at J (for the right margin).
What we have said about
working the edging applies
equally to the insertion; set
pins, if you find it useful,
where the plaits cross, and set pins inside the loops
and curves to keep them in shape.

No. 35.—*Edging for Round D'Oyley*

This is a useful edging for a round d'oyley. It requires eighteen pairs of bobbins, wound in pairs

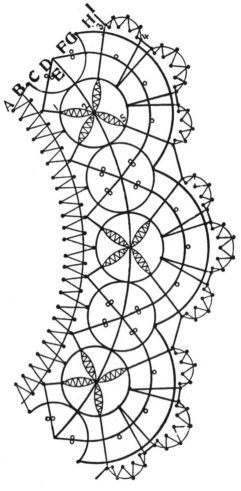

with Mecklenburg thread No. 6. Our pattern is a quarter of the whole; the tracings must be fitted

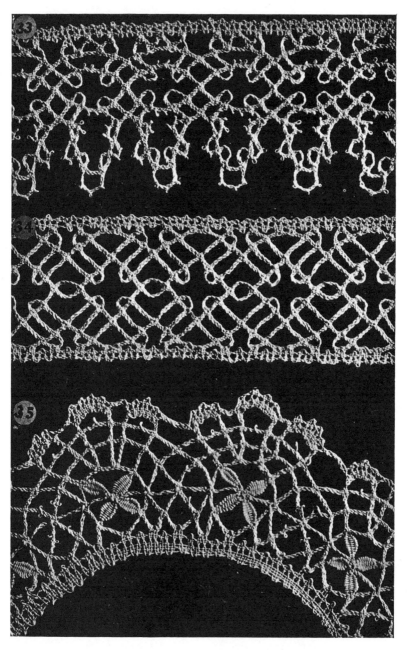

No. 33. PLAITED EDGING (AFTER "LE POMPE")
No. 34. PLAITED INSERTION (AFTER "LE POMPE")
No. 35. PLAITED EDGING FOR ROUND D'OYLEY

No. 36. PLAITED INSERTION WITH CORNER, AND DOUBLE INSERTION (reduced)

carefully to one another so that they complete the circle accurately. Hang three pairs at A, one at B (these are for the margin), two each at C, D, E, F, G, H, I. Begin making the plaits and intersections in the usual way. At 1, make a petal; at 2, take the plait through it and set a pin; leave the pairs of the plait hanging, make another petal, and then the intersections with the plaits from F, H, and I. From 3 with the four pairs of the plaits make a little curved band of c.s., twisting the workers between the outer passives and the other two, till you come to 4; from 4, two plaits start again. The other two curves of the scallop are made in the same way. When the plait of the scallop is brought back to 5, its threads are formed into a petal. Take the pairs of the plait hanging from 2 through the petal, take out the pin at 2 and set it again below these four pairs; make the left two into a petal, and plait the right two very tightly, so as to keep the centre of the flower well in place. The rest of the working is quite obvious. On completing the circle, the finishing off is done in the usual way by threading the loose ends into the loops where the bobbins were hung on and fastening them neatly.

No. 36.—*Cornered Insertion*

This insertion is quickly made, and wears well. It is very handsome in pillow-cases, especially over an underslip of coloured linen; the sheets could then be trimmed with No. 37 to match. It would trim table linen or a linen dress, white underskirt, etc.

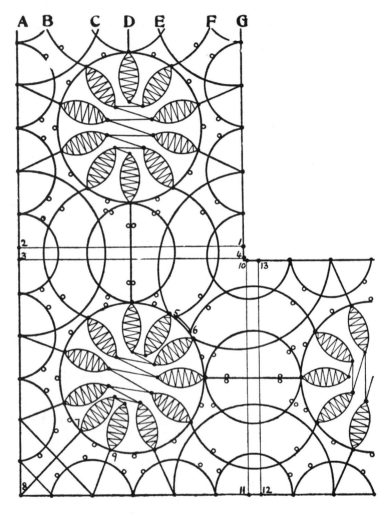

Harris's No. 25 2-cord thread ; twenty-two pair of bobbins, with six extra pair for the corners. Hang on two pair at A, D, G, four at B, C, E, F. The course of the bobbins is too simple to need much explanation. At 1 take one pair from the right-hand edge straight across all the plaits in c.s., twisting it twice between each pin. From 2 to 3 form a plait of three pair for the left-hand edge, and then bring the single pair straight across to its own border again.

From 5 to 6 there must be a plait of four (indicated in the pattern by a double line). Add four pair below 6 for the leaf and one of the plaits, and another two pair to form the extra leaf 7, cutting them out at the corner 8. Cut out four more pair at 9. Points 10, 11, 12, 13 in the same way as 1, 2, 3, 4. Here the pattern begins again.

The double insertion takes only forty-two pairs, the two edges being merged at the middle. The connecting cross line 1—2 is here formed by a plait instead of a single pair, obtained by borrowing one pair from the first plait which crosses it after 1. This pair is returned to its old place on the way back just before 4. Otherwise the working is the same in both cases, and the effect of the double pattern is far richer.

No. 37.—Edging to match No. 36

Harris's No. 25 2-cord thread. Hang two pair at A, D, four at B, C, E, F, G, H, twenty-eight pair in all.

From 1—2, 3—4, 5—8, 6—7 the plaits are of four pair (indicated by double lines), otherwise they are always simple plaits, and their course can easily be followed in the diagram.

Instead of a single pair being taken across from

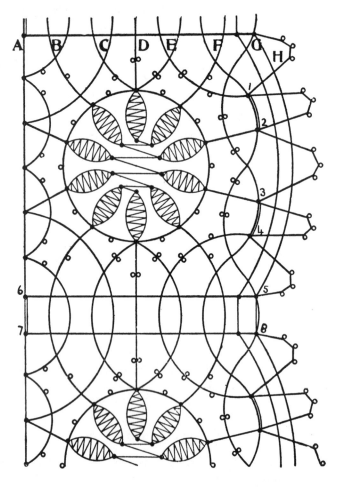

5—6, as was the case in the last insertion, the plait usually forming the outer scallops serves the same purpose.

No. 37. Plaited Lace
No. 38. Curved Lace to match

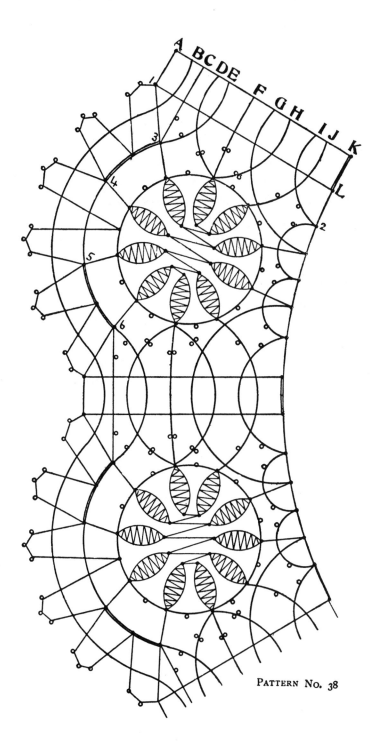

PATTERN No. 38

No. 38.—*Round Table-centre*

This is a slightly simplified version of No. 37, fitted to a curve on the principles laid down on p. 74. The table-centre when finished will be 15 in. in diameter and show twelve repeats of the pattern. The round of linen should be embroidered heavily with Moravian cotton in padded satin stitch. If left plain, it would make a good mat for the basin on the washstand.

Harris's No. 25 2-cord thread; twenty-four pair, four at A, two each at every point from B to K.

Start at A with a plait crossing all the other pairs. From K to L make a plait of four. At L separate and bring a plait across to 1, taking the other on to 2. Other plaits of four are needed from 3—4, and again from 5—6.

No. 39.—*Insertion*

This insertion is a French model from the district of Le Puy. It is easily and quickly worked, and is strong and firm enough for most purposes despite its very open appearance.

Wind twenty-six pairs with Mecklenburg thread 6; hang five pairs at A and E, six at B and D, four at C. Start the edges at A and E in simple c.s. At 1 and 2 on each side bring out two pairs in a plait to help to form the thicker part of the star. These plaits return to their respective borders at 3 and 4. From 5 and 6 start the two upper rays of the star; the diagram shows where plaits are taken in and left out.

At 7 cross the two pairs of workers without twisting.
At the base of these rays, the two pairs on each side
nearest the border go to
start the two middle rays
on the right and left; the
two centre pairs come down
to the ring in a plait, and
the remaining six pairs
singly. It is best to set
pins between the threads
of these pairs, in order to
force back the workers of
the rays and separate the
c.s. of the rays well from
that of the central ring.
After 8, return your workers only through two pair
of passives to make the
right side of the ring; for
the left side, start with the
right of the other three
pairs as workers. At 9,
twist the workers twice,
and cross them with the
workers of the right middle
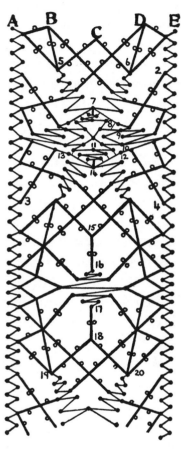
ray, which are not to be twisted ; similarly at 10
and at the two corresponding points of the opposite side. At 11 let the workers and the left pair of
passives of the right side hang over a pin, and take
the workers of the left side the whole way across. At
12 and 13 cross your workers with the last pair of

passives, which take their place. At 14 take one pair
of the plait into the c.s. of the rays on each side, and
cross the workers of the two rays. From 15 to 16
make a plait of four pairs. At 16 begins a h.s.
lozenge.

Make two picots facing each other in the middle of
each longer line, one only in each shorter line.

No. 40.—*Square (see Sheet* 1)

This square is for one of the chequered bedspreads
in vogue, where it might alternate with the Russian
square No. 7 and with squares of filet guipure. It is
quickly worked, and for its size takes a relatively
small number of bobbins, twenty-six pair.

Thread, Harris's No. 25 (2-cord). Hang four pair
at A, C, E, two at B, F, G, eight at D.

Begin at A, bringing one plait round the circle
B C, etc., until it eventually reaches A again, to
which point it is fastened by a sewing. The other
plait from A goes straight to 2, crossing those that
start from B, C, D. Begin the border at D. Of the
eight pair at D, two form a plait, three are passives in
the cloth, two form the outer edge, as in No. 11, and
the remaining pair are the workers, twisted between
the 3 passives and the outer edge. At 1 the workers
are caught into the plaited circle and return to the
border. At 2 the plait from A touches the border,
goes out to 3, to which point it is fastened by a picot,
and returns to the border at 4. Thence it goes to E,
where the border workers again join it and then

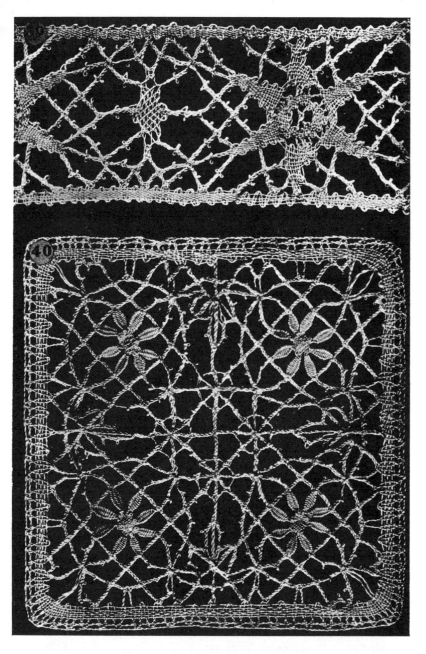

No. 39.   Plaited Insertion
No. 40.   Plaited Square (reduced)

No. 41. PLAITED TRIANGLE (reduced)

return. Pairs for two new plaits are hung in at this
point. The old plait goes on to 5, 6, 7 (as points
2—4), and thence back to the circle.

Now form your flower with the plaits coming from
C and E; 8 is like 1; at 9 the plait from D,
having touched the border, sends out a single pair to
touch the circle and return again to 9. The plaits at
10 and 12 are looped in a similar way to the point
of intersection 11. At F hang in two new pair for
the plait F—11.

At 13 you will have three plaits at your disposal;
take one back to A, thence to 14, and up again to 16.
With the other two make a plait of four from 13 to 15.
At 15 take a single pair out to either side and continue a simple plait from 15 to 17, where the single
pairs forming the small circle come in again to form a
plait of four pairs. At 18 two of these start the second
plaited circle; the other two go to form petal *a*.

These circles resemble one another too much to
need fresh explanation. Sewings are required at 19
and 18, 20 and 21, and the corresponding points in
the last circle.

At G the last two pair are hung in. At 23, the corresponding point on the third side, two pair are cut
out; this difference necessitates a sewing at 22 to
attach the loop of plait at 24, and the same at 25.

Cut out two pair at 26, four pair at 14, fasten the
single pairs of the last small circle to the existing
plait by sewings at 27 and 28. Knot off the plait of
four at 13, and the other plaits one at B, two at C,
the rest at D.

This knotting off must be done after the last stitch has been made, the pins all removed, and the lace turned over on the wrong side.

No. 41.—*Triangle* (*see Sheet* 1)

This triangle forms a handsome and solid ornament for the corners of a pillow-case or cloth. Its only real difficulty consists in the number of bobbins, a difficulty inherent in almost all pillow-lace triangles except those of Russian lace.

D.M.C. thread No. 30; fifty-eight pair. Hang on six pair at X and add one pair to the middle of each row of c.s., so that by the time you reach A there are fourteen pair; after that add one pair to every other row, so that by the time you reach B forty-four more pair have been added, to supply the twenty-two further plaits which start from this side. Adding pairs to a thick c.s. border like this one is a simple matter. Hang each additional pair to a pin outside the pattern, and a couple of inches above the place where it is to be added. Work your c.s. as usual and take the additionals in in the middle of the braid. When the lace is finished, with a pair of sharp scissors cut off the ends of thread flush with the braid.

From A cross only six pair of passives in your c.s., take out two of these at 1 for the plait. At 2, with the right-hand pair of the remaining passives as workers, c.s. across two more pair. At 3, with the left-hand pair as workers, c.s. across the two last pair. Unite these two narrow bands of c.s. by a whole-stitch at 4, 5, etc., all down this side.

The plaits starting from the right side are only caught into the left border. At 7, with the plaits from 1 and 6, begin the right and left semicircle of petals, taking the other plaits through them between each pair of petals to meet in the centre of the flower, which starts in h.s. at 8. At 9 the pairs forming the petals meet again, and start a c.s. lozenge fed by the other plaits. Down the centre of the lozenge is a row of openwork formed by twisting the workers once each time they pass between the two middle pairs of passives.

The other flowers and lozenges are worked in the same way, being fed by the fresh plaits that come from the right.

At 10 set a pin to terminate the petal, continue in a plait to 11, take this into the border passives, form the corner as p. 93. At 12 take out the plait again to 10, fasten it there by a sewing, and continue your petals as usual.

From C onwards to 14 cut out two pair from the middle of the border every time that a fresh plait enters it. A plait from 13 goes to the border. At 14 take the plait into the border and out again at 15 to join the flower at 16, where it is knotted off. After 15 cut out the pairs as before. At 17 take in the three pairs of the first half of the left-hand border, and at 18 those of the second. At 19 cease weaving, cut all the threads, wind the workers tightly two or three times round the passives in reverse directions. Knot them firmly, and cut off all the ends neatly.

CHAPTER XI

SAXONY GUIPURE

Ach wenn er nur käm
Und mich emal nähm,
    Damit ich doch endlich vom Klöppelsack käm !
      *   *   *
Jetzt is er gekomme
Und hat mich genomme,
    Jetzt bin ich nur ferner an'n Klöppelsack komme.
         —SAXONY FOLKSONG.[1]

THE guipures of this chapter have little or nothing geometrical about them. One pattern, it is true (No. 46), is of Arabesque scroll work, somewhat akin to a geometrical design, but all the others are attempts at a rendering more or less free of leaves, roses, "pines," palms, hearts, vine-leaves, and pansies.

While the designs are complex, the technical elements which go to build them up are of the simplest. There is no variety of grounds as in Torchon, or of "modes and fillings" as in Honiton. The figures of c.s. and h.s. are joined together by simple plaits and twists. These are coarse laces, most unjustly despised by the professional worker, and admirably suited for the amateur, who wastes neither time nor

[1] Its age has not made the Saxony lace trade respected. The boy from the Erzgebirge who taught us our first stitches would have scorned to know more than the elements. He said only poor people *made* lace, he dealt in it. And the heroine of the song shares the same opinion. If only she could marry she would get rid of her lace pillow, and when she marries she only has to work at it the harder.

eyesight in making them. The patterns are all effective, the finer ones discreetly so, as becomes a dress
or handkerchief, the coarse ones boldly, as is needed
in house decorations, large covers, window curtains,
sheets, pillows, and table linen.

We have called these laces Saxony guipures for the
good reason that nearly all the models come from
Saxony, or just across the border in Bohemia. One,
it is true, is French ; perhaps a Frenchwoman would
think the chapter better named Le Puy guipure, and an
Italian, Rapallese lace. But in these days, when it is
the habit to sneer at German art and to question the
workmanship of anything made in Germany, let us
be fair to the Vaterland and not be ashamed to
acknowledge our indebtedness.

These laces introduce no new technical points.
Any one who has worked through chapters ix and x
will find few difficulties beyond the greater number of
bobbins to control. But no one should begin on this
chapter without at least having mastered chapter ix.

The great point in working Saxony guipures is to
see that as many threads enter your "mat" as must
go out of it. Once those numbers cease to correspond, not only is one part of the lace overcrowded,
but another is impoverished. Still, there is no
need to be over-conscientious, and undo large pieces
of work because of some such slip ; a little ingenuity
will generally bring back the erring bobbins into
place. In our diagrams the connecting plaits are
indicated by thick lines, the simple twists of two
threads by finer ones.

No. 42.—*Insertion*

This insertion, composed of large flowers in half-stitch connected by plaits, is simple to work and very effective. It should be worked in Mecklenburg thread No. 6, and requires twenty-four pairs. Hang four pairs at A, two each at letters B to K. The margins are the same as No. 29. Each time twist the pair of F but not the pairs of E, and twist the workers between the pair of F and the nearest pair of E, but not between the two pairs of E. At 1, 4, connect with plaits from D and I respectively.

Plait the pairs of B, C, G, H, making picots, also the pairs at 1 and 4. Proceed to work the flower in half-stitch, beginning with the left of the four pairs of A, and working in the direction of the lines in the diagram. One pair of the plait from G must be taken in at 5, the other at 7; one pair of the plait from B at 6 and the other at 8, and similarly with the plaits from H, C, 4 and 1, as the diagram shows. On setting pin 9 you will have sixteen pairs in the width of the flower. With the pair hanging to the right of pin 9, work through the next eight pairs, set pin 10; h.s. below the pin. Of the two pairs making this h.s., work the right one back through six pairs (the remaining one being hung up at pin 9) and set pin 11; here leave off another pair, which is to be plaited with the pair of 9. Continue the half-stitches to 12, where a pair is hung up, and on to 13. Now take the other pair of 10, work it h.s. through the seven pairs on the left to 14, and continue like the

other side, leaving off a pair at each of the points 10,
14, 15, 16, 17, till you come to 18.

Plait the pairs left off at 9 and 11, also the pairs
left off at 14 and 16, connect with the margins at 20

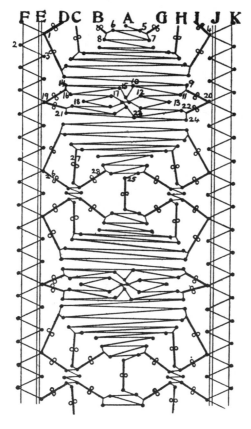

and 19 respectively and plait again (always remembering the picots). Next, the pairs from 10, 15,
12, 17 must be twisted twice, and with them work the
tiny lozenge of cloth-stitch forming the centre of the
flower; the diagram shows where the pairs are taken

in and left off again. Twist the pairs twice as they are left off.

Now continue the half-stitches, taking in pairs where shown, from 18 to 23 and from 13 to 23; at 23 the workers from 21 and 22 are combined, exactly as in lace 11. Thence work to 24, and continue the flower, following the line in the diagram and hanging up pairs where indicated for the plaits. When the flower is completed you will have four pairs left at 25; plait these as described on p. 181.

The plaits numbered 26, 27, 28 are worked into an oval of cloth-stitch, as the diagram shows, and similarly on the other side. This completes a "repeat" of the pattern.

No. 43.—Lace

This beautiful lace appeared in "La Mode Pratique" of 1899, No. 27, and is here reproduced by the kind permission of Messrs. Hachette & Co. It requires thirty-two pairs of bobbins and Mecklenburg thread No. 8, or if preferred it may be worked rather coarser with No. 6. The heart of the flower is worked in half-stitch, the five petals and the stem in cloth-stitch, the broad leaf half in cloth-stitch, half in half-stitch.

Hang one pair at A, two at B and C, three at D, E, and F, two at G, H, I, J, K, L, one at M, three at N, two at O. The thick lines connecting the "mats" are plaits; the thin ones are a single pair twisted from two to four times, according to the length, and the diagram shows clearly where they are taken in and out.

Take one pair of C as the workers of the margin, and work to 1; leave the margin. With one pair of F as workers, and the three pairs of E and one of D as passives, begin the c.s. stem. At 2 connect the

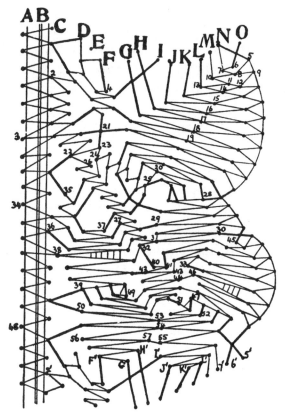

workers of the stem and the workers of the margin, and the same at the four following points on the inside of the margin. On reaching 3, leave the stem and margin.

Work the plaits from I, H, G, F, and make the oval of c.s., beginning at 4. Make the plaits coming

out from it, and also the plaits from J, K, L, N, O.
At 5 the left pair is twisted and combined in c.s. with
the workers of the leaf at 8, then twisted again and
combined with the right pair of 5 (twisted) at 9, and
so on along the edge.

For the leaf, take one pair of 6 as workers, the
other and the pair of N as passives ; c.s. to 7, then
to 8 (where combine, as we have said, with the pair
from 5). Leave off a pair at 8; c.s. to 10 (taking in
pair from M), then to 11 ; here leave off a pair, and
back to 13. With the pairs left off at 11 and 8, h.s.
and connect with the pair from 9 at 12. H.s.
from 12 to 14, and c.s. from 13 to 14, combine the
workers, and so on. The right half is h.s., the left
half c.s., and a pair must be left out from the cloth-
stitches below pins 14, 15, 16, 17, 18, 19, and taken
in to the half-stitches (but not at the succeeding pins
down the middle of the leaf). You can only work
the leaf as far as 20.

Now make the intersecting plaits at 21, and go on
with the stem and the margin. After 23 the stem
branches into two. With the workers from 23, c.s.
through three pairs only to 24, and so on down the
right-hand branch of the stem, taking in and leaving
out pairs as indicated. There will be five pairs remaining at 22 ; take the left-hand as workers, c.s. to
26, and so on down the left-hand branch as far as 27.
Now you can finish the h.s. side of the leaf, taking in
the plait from 25. All the pairs from the h.s. side are
now plaited two by two, and these plaits go to make
the first petal of the flower, beginning with the right

No. 42. GUIPURE INSERTION
No. 43. GUIPURE LACE

pair of 28, and connecting with the margin. At 29, 30, leave off two pairs, then leave the petal and continue the stem from 27, taking in the plait from 29 and connecting with the workers of the petal at 31 ; finish the stem at 32 and the petal at 33.

Go back to the margin from its last point of connection with the stem, and work to 34 (connecting with the plait from 22). Now work the small "mat" of c.s. from 35 to 36, connecting with the workers of the margin. When that is complete you are ready for the left petal beginning at 37 ; connect with the margin at 38. On working from 38, c.s. in the usual way with the first four pairs of passives, but the next six pairs of passives are each *twisted* once before making the c.s., so as to make a line of openwork across the petal. After that continue the c.s. (without twistings) in the usual way to 39.

Next work the heart of the flower in h.s., beginning from 40 ; take in plaits at 41, 42, and a pair at 43, and leave off pairs at 44 and the following points as shown.

Begin the second petal on the right at 45, connect with the margin as you did in making the leaf. On working from 46, the four middle pairs of passives must be twisted to make a line of openwork as in the left-hand petal. The petal ends at 47.

Work the margin from 38 to 48. Then the petal from 49 to 50, and the last one from 51 to 52. After that, the workers of the two petals are combined at 53 and 54, and at each of these pins a pair is left off from the left petal and taken into the right one ; at 55 a pair is left off from the right one and taken into

the left at 57.   At 56 and the next point, two pairs
each are left off to form the passives of the stem in
the next repeat ; a pair from F′ are the workers.
To show more clearly where the repeat begins, we
have marked some of the points corresponding to the
starting points with the same letters dotted.

No. 44.—Handkerchief Border

This pattern would also make a pretty square
d'oyley if only one repeat were worked between each
two corners.   It lends itself well to working in silk.
D.M.C. thread No. 45 ; 28 pair.   Hang thirteen pair
at A, two at B, C, eight at D, three at E.

With the left-hand pair at A make c.s. across all the
other pairs.   At 1 take out two pairs to form first a
plait, then the leaf, then a plait again, crossed by the
leaves from B and C, and taken at last into the lower
band of cloth at 2.

At 3 leave the lower band and begin again at 1.
Form the curve at 4 as explained in the chapter on
Russian lace, p. 92.   After 5 return to the lower
band ; from 6 take out a pair which, twisted twice
between each pin, crosses the three pairs from the
upper band in whole-stitch, and is taken into the
latter at 7.   The second and third scallops are made
in practically the same way as the first.   The rest is
Torchon work, indicated clearly enough in the
diagram ; the lozenges are c.s.

The corner of this handkerchief has the great advantage of needing no additional bobbins.   In order
to start the central mat of c.s., take out a plait of three

pair from 8, leaving a pair hanging at 9 to form the
junction with the returning band.   All pairs on the

right are taken into this mat, all those on the left and
at the bottom are taken out.

No. 45.—*Tie* (*see Sheet* 2)

This is not a formidable piece of work ; the length of the explanation is due to the variety in the lace, which at the same time makes it pleasant to work.

Barbour's thread No. 80 3-cord ; forty-three pairs are needed at the widest part, twenty-eight for the narrow band that forms the length of the tie.

Hang on six pair at A as two plaits of three linked together at A and parting to right and left. At 1 and 2 bring out one pair to left and right respectively. Continue the two plaits (now of two pair each) to 3 and 4. Hang on four pair at B in the same way as at A, taking them down to join the leaf in two plaits entering at 5 and 7. In like manner four pair at C, D.

Start the c.s. leaf from 3 with the left-hand pair from A as workers across the others from A and two from C as passives. Leave the workers at 4. Start again at 5 with the right-hand pair of the first plait from B as workers across all the rest, including the old workers left at 4.

At 6 take out the edge plait for the right-hand side; the edge is like No. 32 above, only the intersecting line is here a twist of one pair, not a plait.

Start again at 7 with the left-hand pair of the second plait from B as workers across all the rest. At 8 make the same operation with the first plait from D. Use the second plait from D for the left-hand edge. At 9 hang in two more pair, also at 10. From 9 cross only six pair of passives, and start the seventh as workers across the remainder. Cross the two pairs of new workers in c.s. at 11 and at the five similar points below. At 12 begin to take out pairs for the leaves below, one at a time, and soon after 12 add two pair in the cloth (see p. 194). At 13 hang in a new pair (wound pair-wise) to take out to the leaf below. At 14 cross the workers in c.s. with one another, set a pin and let them fall to left and right of it, then take the left-hand pair of passives from the right side as workers for the rest of the leaf. At 15 hang in a new pair to take out to the leaf below. Finish the leaf with a little plait.

Hang in two pair at 16 and work c.s. down the leaf, adding two more pair before 17 and two more before 18. Stop here and begin at 19.

Add two pair at 19 and another one before 20. At 21 cross the workers of the left leaf with the workers of the right leaf, and finish the leaf with the right workers.

Start at 22, adding two pair; add two more at 23, taking them out in a plait of four to the leaf below. Stop at 24, and begin on the opposite side at the corresponding leaf.

Add two pair. Take out a pair to the leaf below at every pinhole on the lower edge save 26 and 27. At 26 take the edge plait into the leaf and let it out again at the pin below. Stop at 27.

Begin again with the edge plait at 26 ; add one pair, which with the pair coming in from the leaf above will start the new leaf. Take in the edge plait again. At 27 cross the workers with those of the leaf above, and stop at 29.

Continue the old leaf from 27, taking the workers across all the passives and the workers of the right side to 24. At 29 cross the workers again with those of the lower leaf.

Begin the leaf starting at 23, add one pair at 30, the last of the additionals. The last three joins to the leaf below are formed by crossing with the workers of that leaf.

The first few stitches of the last leaves to right and left are made by one pair from the leaf above crossing the two pairs of the edge plait until enough fresh pairs come down from the leaf above to form the passives.

At 30 and 31 the joins are made by taking pairs from the *lower* leaves to the upper. After 29 change cloth-stitch for half-stitch. Exactly below 32 change back to c.s. and finish the bottom of the last right-hand leaf; at the same point on the return resume the h.s.

At 33 and 34, the base of the two scallops, cut out the two middle pairs of passives on either side; there is no need to knot them off, as the work is close and firm at these points.

From 35 take the workers across only ten pairs of passives to 36 and back again, taking out two pairs at every left-hand pin until 38 inclusive. Cut out a pair at 39. Stop at 40.

Start again in h.s. from right to left above 36, taking out petals, as indicated in the diagram, until 41 inclusive. Cut out a pair at 42.

Finish the sunflower.

Start again at 40 in h.s., taking in the petals of the sunflower. Cut off one pair at 43, 44, and 45. On

No. 45. Guipure Lace Tie

reaching 46 let the workers hang over a pin and begin again at 42. When you get back to 46 take the workers of the right side across both workers and passives of the left. End the ring with a plait at 47.

The two following leaves present no difficulties. When they are finished cut out three pair at the base of the right-hand leaf and two pair at the base of the left. It is best to cut them separately, taking the pair lying between two pairs that are to form a plait going to the leaf below. The tightening of the plait prevents the ends of thread from showing, if you cut them off closely, and no further knotting off is needed.

Between these two leaves and starting from point 48 is a tiny diamond of Torchon ground work. The two pairs coming from the lowest point of the diamond are the workers for the new pair of leaves. At the lowest point of the left-hand leaf cut out one pair. By now you will have reduced your bobbins to twenty-eight pair, which is the number needed for the whole middle part of the tie.

The last leaf is worked in much the same way as the first. At 49 start the fourth pair of passives (counting from the left) as workers towards the left. On each side of the leaf there is one point where the respective workers cross those of the border. Leave the right-hand workers hanging across a pin at 50 and take the left-hand workers across the whole leaf.

The border consists of four pair for h.s. and two for c.s. to give a firmness to the edge. Each plait of the centre part has a picot half-way between each two points of intersection.

The small medallions which vary the band are made very much in the same way as the large one at the ends. After point 51, where the third plait from the right-hand border enters the medallion, take your workers only across six pair and return. At 53 and 54 bring out pairs well twisted to join the flower, taking them back directly after they have been crossed with the workers of the flower. Start the left side at 52. At 55 leave the right workers and the second pair from the leaf hanging over a pin, and finish the ring with the left workers.

In the original tie there are six repeats of medallions, but of course the length can be altered to taste. To work the further end, everything in the instructions must be reversed; the pattern must be turned upside down, and wherever bobbins were cut away before, they must be added, and where they were added, cut away.

No. 46.—*Cornered Insertion*

This model is very suitable for large square pillow-cases, tea-cloths or even window curtains.

Forty-eight pair are needed with six pair of additionals for the corner, and D.M.C. thread No. 25.

Hang on three pair at A, R, five at B, Q, two at C, E, G, H, I, J, L, M, P, one at F, N, four at D, K, O.

The only difficulty in this pattern is the manipulation of so many bobbins. The diagram needs very little explanation. For the working of the c.s. rings round the spiders with first one pair of workers, then

PATTERN No. 46

two, then one to finish, go on the same principle as in the medallions for the tie No. 45.

Add two pair each at 1, 2 and 3 ; and cut out two pair each at 4, 5 and 6.

Turning the curve of h.s. at 7, it will be necessary to use the Russian curve (p. 92.)

No. 47.—Broad Lace (see Sheet 2)

This lace is very suitable for trimming sheets or window curtains. It is firm and strong in the fabric, and would bear endless washings. Its only drawback is that five additional pairs are hung in and out at each repeat, to help form the broadest part.

D.M.C. thread No. 20 ; fifty-seven pair. Hang four at A, two at B, D, E, F, G, I, J, eleven at C, seventeen at H, and six at K.

Begin working c.s. with the right-hand of the pairs at H. After point 2, return across only eight of them, and start the left-hand pair of the remaining ten as workers across the rest from 3. At 4 cross the two pairs of workers with each other in c.s. At 5 set a pin and let the workers hang to the left of it and the last pair of passives to the right.

Start in c.s. below C. After 6 return across only ten pair of passives ; point 7 as point 3. At 9 hang on two additionals for the plait. After 11 take your workers not only across all the passives, but across the four plaits coming in from above, across the old workers and passives left at pin 5, and across one further pair of passives from the right side. Then take these latter as workers and return across the

No. 46. Guipure Insertion with Corner

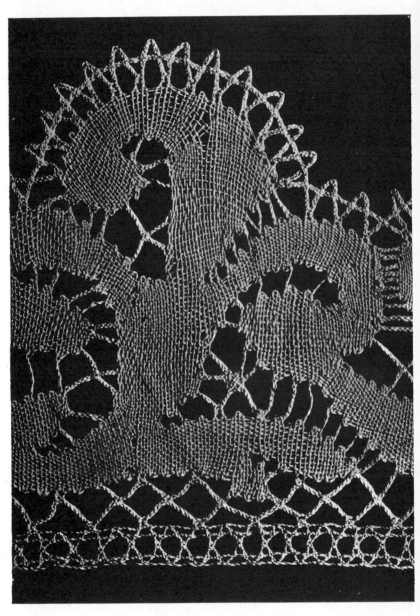

No. 47.   Broad Guipure Lace

passives coming from the plaits, and across those of the left side that came in at 8 and 10.

Return with the last of these passives as workers; take in three more pair at the right, and return again with the last pair of these as workers. Take the old workers in c.s. across one further pair of passives to the right. From 15 continue in the usual way.

Point 16 as point 3, likewise point 17.

Begin at 18; at 19 hang on two new pairs and one at 20. Point 21 as 3. At 22 take in the plait from above, and continue to the right till you can take in the workers of the middle part of the leaf at pin 23. Now to 24, taking in only two pairs of the passives of the left side of the leaf, using the second of these as workers on the return journey, which goes straight across all the passives to 25. At 26 change your workers for the next pair of passives.

With the right pair at 27, c.s. to the left across three other pairs. Then with the last of these, c.s. across the right pair of 27 and one other. With this last, c.s. across the one that has just crossed it, and pass on to 28. At 28, as at 26, change your workers for the next pair of passives. From 28 you cross only so far as 29, leaving all save two pair of the passives coming from the centre part to your right. Make c.s. with your last pair of workers and the next pair of passives on the left at 30; stop here.

Point 33 as 3; six pairs of the passives to the right go to make the three plaits. After the c.s. junction at 29 you can complete the left part of the leaf, taking the workers straight across all the other pairs to 31. Cut out five pairs and finish with a plait at 32.

Continue the other part from 29 to 34, then start at 35. At 36 leave out three pairs, at 37 three more, at 38 three more. At 39 set a pin and let the workers fall to the left of it, the last pair of passives to the right. Start again at 34, taking in the pair from the upper part, and finish the leaf with the workers from 38.

From 36 start again in simple c.s. At 40 the repeat of the pattern ends.

No. 48.—*Broad Insertion* (*see Sheet* 2)

This insertion, used in conjunction with the lace No. 47, would make a handsome pair of curtains. It would also make panels down the brise-bise to match, on sideboard cloths or sofa backs, or trim the side of a pillow-case. Its only real difficulties are the number of bobbins needed and the piece of raised work on the pine, which is really more fidgeting than difficult. It takes quite a short time to make, and is most interesting in the working.

Thread, Harris's No. 25 3-cord; fifty pair. Hang four at A, D, E, O, two at B, C, F, G, I, J, M, three at K, six at N, five at L, six at H.

Start at L in c.s., taking in and giving out pairs as shown in the diagram. After 1 begin the border at O, which is made like the Russian braid No. 9 on p. 92. After 2 begin at J in c.s. across the pairs of K; finish the leaf by a plait at 3.

Start with the left plait from H across the plaits

from G, F, E.   After 4 cross only six pair (including the pair taken in at 4); take one out at 5, stop at 6.

Start again at 7 with the sixth pair of the remaining passives as workers across those further to the left. Before 8 work the plaits from B, C, and the border from A as far as 9.

Start at 10 with one pair of the plait as workers across the other three loose pairs twisted twice.   At 6 cross your workers in c.s. with those of the central leaf to the right and return.   The workers of the central leaf return in half-stitch.   At 11 both workers meet again in the same way.   Continue your h.s. to 12 and start on a fresh leaf at 13.   All these three leaves must be worked together in the way indicated, as also the fourth, which starts at 14.   After the h.s. mat is finished, the remaining joins between the leaves, where they are not made by taking out plaits or pairs, are formed of a single whole-stitch, in which the two pairs of workers are exchanged.

At 15, after attaching the plait by a c.s., cross only two pair of passives with your workers and start another pair at 16, which will also have two pair of passives on which to operate.   The joins 17, 18, etc. are made by whole-stitches as above.

At 9 the left-hand stem is attached to the border by c.s. of its workers with the border workers, the latter twisted twice.   Plaits of three are needed from 19 to 20 and 21 to 22.   The solid work at 20 and 22 is c.s.   The plaits of three go out again opposite the points at which they entered.

Begin the pine in h.s. at 23. Work to 24, set a pin there, and leave the workers and the last pair of passives hanging on either side of it. Do the same at 26. Then take the workers of the leaf which starts at 27 to finish all three leaves. After 28 return across only six pairs of passives. At 29 begin working c.s.

Work the mat starting at 30 in c.s. At 31 cross only four pair of passives, and start a fresh pair of workers at 32. Take your workers out in the plait at 33, and continue with those coming from 29. Stop at 34.

Begin again at 35 with the left-hand pair across three pair of passives in h.s. Stop at 36 as at 24.

Begin at 37 and work down, taking in all the pairs from the leaf above, including those at 36. Leave out four pair at 41 to start the last leaf of the pine. Stop at 38.

You are now ready for the centre of the pine. After 39 take the second and third pairs of passives and throw them back over the pillow out of your way. Do the same with the last pair save two before 40, and the fourth and fifth pair after 43.

Start the leaf at 41 and work it together with the centre, making two joins in whole-stitch. From 42 begin taking out pairs as indicated from the centre to this leaf. Stop when there are three pairs of passives left between you and point 44.

With the two pair left near 40 form a leaf, and with those at 39 form a plait to meet it. Unite them at pin 45 in a single c.s. (see p. 182); with the two right-hand pairs continue the plait; with the others

No. 48. Broad Guipure Insertion (reduced)

No. 44. Guipure Handkerchief Border
No. 49. Guipure D'oyley Border

make another leaf and take this into the h.s. at the point already reached before 44.

Meanwhile the fourth and fifth pairs after 43 have been laid aside in the same way as those near 40, and are taken in again as third and fourth after 46 (not counting the two pair taken out at that point to form the plait). In the same way the fourth and fifth pairs after 47 are taken out and brought in again as fifth and sixth after 48. Points 49 and 50 as 45. At 51 transform your plait into a leaf and take it into the h.s. as fourth and fifth pairs after 52.

At 53 change h.s. to c.s. There are no further difficulties.

The repeat of the pattern ends with the pine, but the following repeat must be reversed, which is quite easy when the pattern has been traced on tracing linen, as the direction lines traced on the face of the material will show through at the back.

No. 49.—*Square D'oyley*

Mecklenburg thread No. 6; twenty-four pair and twelve pair of additionals for the corners.

Hang five at A, four at B, two at C, D, E, F, H, I, three at G. There is no peculiarity in the working until you reach 1. Here hang in two new pairs, and with these and the four pairs of the stems and two plaits from the leaf, work as if you were finishing a spider (p. 125). When finished, take the two centre pair down in a plait, and use the other four on either side to start the outline of the heart to right and left in cloth-stitch. Add two

more pair at 2, 3, 4, and four at 5. All these
additionals being introduced in the cloth, it is not
necessary to wind them double ; follow the method

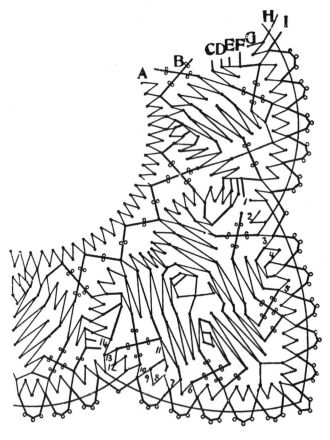

described on page 194, and cut them out in the same
way at 6, 7, 8, 9, and 10.

The joins in the flower, unless formed by plaits and
pairs, are single whole-stitches. Cut out a pair from
the base of the petal at 11. Take out one pair from
the c.s. at 12 and two at 13 to start the new stem.

Cross both pairs of workers in c.s. through the pairs of the plait at 14, and finish off the heart spider-fashion in the way it began. One pair must be cut from the bottom of the spider, and you will then again have twenty-four pair with which to start the next quarter of the d'oyley.

No. 50.—*Handkerchief Border* (*see Sheet 2*)

Thread, Barbour's No. 80 3-cord. Twenty-eight pair are needed to start with; later on as many as forty-seven in all.

Hang on four pair at A, F, three at B, two at C, nine at D, six at E. After working a little of the edge plaits from A, start at D. The two pair to the left form a plait joining the h.s. hexagon at 1; the five central pairs form a band of c.s. coming in at 2, the remaining two pair a plait passing away to the right. Start the leaf and two plaits from E. Just above 5 the junction of three plaits is made by a cloth-stitch, treating three bobbins as one.

You will now be ready for the hexagon, beginning from below C. Just before 3 take the two left-hand of the last three pair and hang them backwards over the pillow out of your way. Do the same with the last two pair save two before 4, and with the third and fourth pairs after 5. Continue the h.s. till you have still two pair left between you and 6; then form the petals *a*, *b*, and *c* of the raised flower. Form the centre as you would a spider (p. 125), and finish the lower petals. Resume your workers and take in petal *d* before 6.   After passing two pair of passives from 7 take in petal *f*, and two pairs before 8 petal *e*. From 9 change to c.s., starting the band with four pair.

At 10 add four pair to the border to start the h.s. leaf. After 11, having passed two pair, throw back two pair over the pillow in reserve for the raised spray. After 12 pass one pair and throw back two ; then pass two again and throw back two more. After 13 pass two pair in h.s. and stop. Resume the reserve pairs and form three leaves, the first ending in a plait ; place one pair from each leaf between both pairs of the plait, set a pin at 14 and tightly plait the rest of the stem. Remove the pin and hang the plait back over the pillow. Resume your h.s., taking in the four pairs of the leaves. Two pairs after 15 take in the stem plait also.

At 16 bring back from the border a plait of three, thus getting rid of the single pair joining the last leaf to the border.

At 17 the c.s. mat starts with five pair. In the h.s. mat to the left of the latter, after passing three pair after 18, throw back two pair for the raised petal. Take them in again four pair after 19. At the bottom of this mat four plaits go down to the next one like it ; the remaining four pair form the c.s. band to the right, with a pair from the next c.s. mat as workers.

Three pairs after 20, turn back two more reserve pairs for a petal, which is taken in again three pairs after 23. At 21 a pair comes in from the nearest c.s.

mat only to go back again at 22.   At 24 the h.s. gives place to a c.s. band of five pair.

After 25 change the c.s. band to h.s.   Throw back the fourth and fifth pairs after 26, and take them in again as fourth and fifth after 27.

At 28 add two pair ; between 29 and 30 gradually add five, and two each at 31 and 32.

Throw back the first two of the last three pairs before 33, also the third and fourth pair after 35. At 34 bring out one pair from the border to join the mat at 35 and then return it to the border at once. The last petal is taken back into the h.s. three pairs after 37, while the stem, after crossing with the last pair at 36, goes out to start the c.s. mat to the left.

Start again in c.s. at 38, adding four pair.   The pair brought out from 54 returns to its own mat immediately.   Go on to 39, then form the five petals between 38 and 39.   Work the c.s. centre of the flower and finish the lower petals.   Take one of these back into the c.s. at 40.

Begin again below 38 with the h.s. mat, taking in a petal at 41.   End the mat with a plait at 42.

At 43 start the corner c.s. mat with the petal there. Leave out one pair each at 43, 44, 45, 46, 47, 48. Form the extreme corner of the leaf Russian fashion (p. 92), and return round the other side, taking in the pairs dropped in order.

At 49 and 50 do not take in the pairs of the petals, but after the work is more advanced cut off the bobbins, bring the threads into place with a needle-

or crochet-hook, and knot them off at the back of the lace.

After finishing the h.s. mat at 51, you will be able to finish off the crescent-shaped c.s. mat left at 40, and then the two small c.s. mats to the left of it.

Begin again at 37.   About 52 cut out, at a little distance from each other, two pair of passives from the border.   Choose them from the original passives (not those newly come in from the h.s.), and there will be no need to knot them off.   Knot off and cut away another pair at 53, and cut away two more about 55 in the narrow part of the c.s.   This reduces your bobbins to the right number again (thirty-two pair) until the narrowing of the pattern, when four more are cut off at the tip of the leaf with the raised work.

At 56 the leaf just begun gives a pair to the c.s. band at the right, receiving back two pair at 57 and one at 58.

No. 50.   Guipure Handkerchief Border

A SHORT BIBLIOGRAPHY OF PILLOW LACE

1. GENERAL HISTORY OF LACE.

   Joseph Séguin. *La Dentelle.* 1875.

   Mrs. Bury Palliser. *History of Lace.* 1865. Second edition edited by A. Dryden and M. Jourdain. 1902.

   Cp. review in the *Quarterly*, July, 1868, pp. 166–188.

   Dreger. *Geschichte der Spitze.* Vienna. 1901.

   A. S. Cole. *Cantor Lectures on the Art of Lace-making.* 1881.

   ——. *Two Lectures on the Art of Lace-making.* Dublin. 1884.

   Albert Ilg. *Geschichte und Terminologie der alten Spitzen.* 1876.

   C. von Braunmühl. Articles in *Kunst und Gewerbe.* Nuremberg. 1882. XVI. p. 33 ff.

   A. Doumert. *La Dentelle.*

   Mrs. E. Neville Jackson. *History of Handmade Lace.* 1900.

2. SPECIAL HISTORIES.

   England. C. C. Channer and M. E. Roberts. *Lace-making in the Midlands, past and present.* 1900.

   Chambers' Repository of useful and amusing tracts. "Lace and Lace-making."

   Italy. G. M. Urbani de Gheltof. *I merletti a Venezia.* 1876. Translated by Lady Layard.

   France. E. Lefébure. *Broderie et Dentelle.* 1887.

   Translated into English, *Embroidery and Lace.* Ed. Cole. 1888.

   A. Lefébure. *Dentelle et Guipure.* Paris. n.d.

   F. Aubry. *La Fabrication de la Dentelle.* Paris. 1854.

   Fabrication de la Dentelle dans le département du Rhône. Lyons. 1862.

   J. Turgan. *Les grandes Usines.* 1866. (On Le Puy Laces, VI. 237.)

Germany. Hugo Fischer. *Technologische Studien im Säch-sischen Erzgebirge.* 1878.

Denmark. Sara Rasmussen. *Klöppelbuch.* Copenhagen. n.d.

Spain. J. F. Riaño. South Kensington Art Handbooks. *The Industrial Arts in Spain.* 1875. pp. 271–276.

Russia. Sophie Davydoff. *La Dentelle Russe.* St. Petersburg.

3. ON THE NATURE AND CLASSIFICATION OF LACES.

A. M. S. *Point and Pillow Lace.* 1889.

Mary Sharp.   ,,   ,,   (second edition of the above). 1905.

Hugo Fischer. Article in *Der Civil Ingenieur.* Freiberg. 1878. Vol. XXIV.

Diderot and D'Alembert. *Encyclopædia,* article " Dentelle."

4. PATTERNS.

OLD PATTERN-BOOKS FOR PILLOW LACE

Le Pompe. I. Venice. 1557 and 1559.
II. Venice 1560 and 1562. Reprinted by F. Paterno. Vienna. 1879.

R. M. *Die Künst der Dentelschnüren.* Zürich. Published about 1550 by Christoff Froschower.

Elisabetta Catanea Parasole. *Teatro delle nobili et virtuose donne.* Rome. 1616. Reprinted by E. Wasmuth. Berlin. 1891.

Mathias Mignerak. *La Pratique de l'Aiguille Industrieuse.* Paris. 1605.

R. Shorleyker. *A Scholehouse for the Needle.* London. 1632.

Bartolomeo Danieli. [A pattern-book of about 1640, wanting title-page, in the Victoria and Albert Museum.]

MODERN PATTERN-BOOKS

Karl Jamnig and Adelheid Richter. *Technik der geklöppelten Spitzen.* Vienna.

Sara Rasmussen. *Klöppelbuch.* Copenhagen. n.d.

Caulfield and Saward. *Dictionary of Needlework.* London. 1881. See especially articles on Guipure, Honiton, Pillow, Saxony Lace.

Les Dentelles aux fuseaux. Published by the lace and embroidery shop "La Boule de Neige." Le Mans. n.d. (1906.)

Tina Frauberger. *Handbuch der Spitzenkunde.* No. 2 of Seemann's "Kunsthandbücher." 1889.

Brigitte Hochfelden. *Das Spitzenklöppeln,* in Ebhardt's "Handarbeiten" series. Berlin. n.d.

Thérèse de Dillmont. *Encyclopedie der weiblichen Handarbeiten.*[1] Published by Dollfus Mieg & Co., threadmakers, Mülhausen. n.d.

Wm. Barbour, threadmaker, Lisburn, Ireland, publishes a series of needlework books which contain a few lace patterns ; also a Torchon handbook.

J. Harris, threadmaker, Cockermouth. *Torchon Lace.* n.d.

Pillow Lace. Needlecraft, No. 40. Published by the Manchester School of Embroidery.

Weldon's *Practical Needlework,* No. 124, "Torchon Lace," and No. 229, "Pillow Lace."

Myra's *Library of Needlework,* No. 40, "Pillow Lace."

C. von Braunmühl. *Das Kunstgewerbe in Frauenhand.* Berlin. 1885.

Adele Voshage. *Das Spitzenklöppeln.* Leipzig. 1895.

Frieda Lipperheide. *Das Spitzenklöppeln.* Berlin. 1898.

HONITON PATTERNS

Mrs. Treadwin. *Antique Point and Honiton Lace.* 1873.

Caulfield and Saward. *Dictionary of Needlework.* London. 1881.

Weldon's *Practical Needlework,* No. 153, "Honiton Lace."

Mme. Goubaud's *Pillow Lace Patterns.* 1871.

PERIODICALS WHICH PUBLISH PILLOW-LACE PATTERNS

La Mode Pratique. Hachette, Paris.

La Corbeille à ouvrage. Hachette, Paris.

Der Bazar. Berlin.

Die Modenwelt. Berlin.

[1] The large edition differs from the small one. There are also abridged translations in English and French.

ANALYSIS OF THE PATTERNS

Edgings.—Russian, Nos. 3, 5, 8 ; Torchon, 11, 13 (with corner), 15 (with corner), 16 (with fringe), 17, 19, 20; Maltese, 21, 23, 25 (waved), 27 ; Plaited, 33, 37 ; Guipure, 43, 47.

Insertions.—Russian, 2, 4 ; Torchon, 12, 14 (with corner), 18 ; Maltese, 22, 24 ; Plaited, 34, 36 (with corner), 39 ; Guipure, 42, 46 (with corner), 48.

Trimmings (neither edging nor insertion).—Russian, 1 ; Maltese, 28.

Corners.—Russian, 10 (handkerchief) ; Torchon, 13 (narrow lace), 14 (narrow insertion), 15 ; Maltese, 26 (handkerchief), 29 (handkerchief) ; Plaited, 36 (insertion) ; Guipure, 44 (handkerchief), 46 (broad insertion), 49 (d'oyley), 50 (handkerchief).

Shaped pieces—

Squares : Russian, 7 ; Maltese, 30, 31 ; Plaited, 40.
Triangles : Russian, 9 ; Plaited, 41.
Round : Russian, 7.
Rounded borders : Plaited, 35, 38.

Ties.—Maltese. 32 ; Guipure, 45 ; tie-end, Russian, 6.

Waved edging.—Maltese, 25.

Fringed edging.—Torchon, 16.

COMPARATIVE SIZES OF THREADS *

THE following are the makers of the threads mentioned in this book :—

Messrs. French, Russell & Co. (successors to J. and W. Taylor), Leicester, makers of the "Mecklenburg" lace-thread, which can be obtained from almost any draper's and fancy-work shop.

Messrs. J. Harris & Sons, Cockermouth. Depôts at 25 Old Bond Street, London, and in Manchester and Birmingham.

Messrs. Wm. Barbour & Son, Lisburn, Ireland.

Messrs. Dollfus Mieg & Co., Mülhausen. Threads obtainable at the principal London fancy-work shops.

We append a table which gives the numbers of threads of these makers which *approximately* correspond :—

"MECKLEN-BURG."	DOLLFUS MIEG & Co.	BARBOUR.		HARRIS.	
		3-CORD.	2-CORD.	3-CORD.	2-CORD.
—	6	—	—	—	—
—	12	—	—	16	—
—	16	25	—	20	—
0	20	30	—	25	16
2	25	40	—	30	20
4	30	50	—	40	25
6	35	70	45	60	40
8	40	80	50	80	50
10	45	100	70	90	60
12	50	120	80	100	70
20	60	—	100	—	90
36	70	—	120	—	100
60	—	—	140	—	120
100	—	—	150	—	140

* Table is now out of date but is reproduced for its historic interest.

ERRATA

Preface, p., vii., line 14. For "Winslow Lace School" read "Winslow (Bucks) Lace Industry."

Ib., line 17. For "handkerchief border" read "tray-cloth border."

Fig. 23, facing p. 52. For Modern "Russian" Lace, etc., read "Flounce 9 inches wide, copied from an antique Roman pillow lace by the Winslow (Bucks) Lace Industry."

GLOSSARY AND INDEX